INTEGRITY
OF
PASTORAL CARE

New Library of Pastoral Care

INTEGRITY
OF
PASTORAL CARE

DAVID LYALL

Published in Great Britain in 2001 by
Society for Promoting Christian Knowledge
Holy Trinity Church
Marylebone Road
London NW1 4DU

British Library Cataloguing-in-Publication Data

A catalogue record for this book is available
from the British Library

ISBN 0-281-05026-0

Typeset by Pioneer Associates, Perthshire
Printed in Great Britain by
The Cromwell Press, Trowbridge, Wiltshire

Contents

Acknowledgements

This book could not have been written without the help and encouragement of many people. First and foremost, I must express my thanks to colleagues in ministry who willingly gave me access to the stories from their own pastoral experience. There was indeed a real embarrassment of riches, and I have been able to include less than half of the material I received. I have learned much from all that I read, and even where material was not published it enriched my thinking and increased my appreciation of the breadth and depth of pastoral care being exercised within the contemporary Church and community. In the interests of confidentiality, the names of all those mentioned in the case material have been changed.

I must also thank my academic colleagues who have read all or part of the manuscript and made many helpful comments. In particular I would like to name Professor Duncan Forrester, Dr Derek Murray, Dr Ian McDonald and Dr Neil Pembroke who have provided me with constructive feedback regarding both the main argument and points of detail. Without their contribution this book would have been much the poorer.

Introduction

A PERSONAL PERSPECTIVE

As an agnostic teenager, I never expected to become a minister. At school I was good at science and, being brought up in a mining community in West Fife, I went to Edinburgh University (mainly because it was the nearest to home) to study for a degree in chemistry. Yet in my first week at university, an event took place which in due course would lead me in a very different direction. In October 1954, there was a mission to the university led by D. T. Niles, the Indian pastor and theologian, then at the height of his powers as a preacher within the liberal evangelical tradition. Amid the secularity of today's university, it is hard to imagine a missioner being given a five-minute slot at the start of Physics 1. But that is what happened, and I suppose it must have made some impact because within a few months I was allowing myself to be dragged along by fellow students to university services and preached into faith by the then university chaplain, David H. C. Read, who baptized and confirmed me before he departed for a pulpit in New York.

As I progressed through my chemistry course, the idea of becoming a minister began to grow within me, at first as a somewhat ridiculous and unacceptable idea but then with an increasing conviction that would not go away. Psychologists would no doubt pick over other things which were going on in my life at that time and find in them reasons for a change in direction. I was beginning to have doubts about whether I wanted to spend my life in a laboratory. I was quite good at the theory, but it was becoming obvious that my gifts did not lie in experimental science. The fact that I survived a three-month-long vacation job purifying an arsenic compound has been cited

ix

by those who know me as incontrovertible evidence for divine providence. I did graduate with a reasonable degree and spent the next two years teaching chemistry. During this time I was accepted as a candidate for the ministry of the Church of Scotland, learned some Greek, earned some money and married Margaret, whom I had met at an SCM conference.

I studied for the ministry in New College, the home of Edinburgh University's Faculty of Divinity. As a group of students we were nearly all male, young, white and would-be ministers of the Church of Scotland, with the addition of some American postgraduates. (In contrast, the present-day Faculty is ecumenical and international, in terms of both staff and students, with equal numbers of women and men. The number of religious studies students, of all faiths and none, is now far in excess of the candidates for ordination.) We were taught by professors with international reputations, though I now think we rather took them for granted. They were nearly all Scottish, and most of them had been parish ministers for a while as well as concurrently acquiring their doctorates. Norman Porteous introduced us to the biblical theology of the Old Testament, helping us to understand it in a non-fundamentalist way as the cradle of the New Testament. James S. Stewart expounded the New Testament to a packed classroom, with a style which combined rigorous critical scholarship with homiletic power and personal grace. John Burleigh helped us to understand the history of the Scottish Church within the far wider experience and history of the world Church. I majored in Systematic Theology with Tom Torrance and John McIntyre. I keep thinking I have moved on from Professor Torrance's own passionate engagement with the theology of Karl Barth, but every now and again I realize how deeply that exposition has influenced me. John McIntyre, equally at home in patristic and modern theology, broadened our horizons and laid a foundation of a theology which was both critical and committed, enabling most of us to continue in ministry in the midst of the theological storms which were about to break.

By this time I was developing a particular interest in pastoral care and theology, but this could not be studied at degree level. Practical Theology was taught by 'Willie' Tindal, a wise minister and church statesman with much pastoral experience, but at the end of the day the lectures were essentially 'hints and tips', required only for budding ministers of the Kirk. There was a sense in which these years at New College marked, culturally and theologically, the end of an era. In my final year, three books were published which were symptomatic of this transition. John Robinson's *Honest to God* (1963) brought to an unsuspecting public, both within and outside the churches, an awareness of the (then) radical theological ideas of Bonhoeffer, Bultmann and Tillich, ideas with which academic theology had been living comfortably for years but which within the uninitiated provoked a range of reactions from outrage to relief. The New Testament section of the New English Bible saw the light of day, its modern language being at least one factor in the wave of liturgical change which has swept through most denominations. Finally, the unexpurgated version of D. H. Lawrence's *Lady Chatterley's Lover* (1960) was published, initiating what some would consider the beginning of the decline in standards of sexual morality and others a welcome openness and freedom from hypocrisy in such matters. It is arguable that the Church and its ministry is still struggling to come to terms with the new theological, liturgical and ethical movements of which these publications were surely a sign rather than a cause.

At the end of my time in New College, I was fortunate to be awarded a scholarship to spend a year at Yale Divinity School. Here I was able to develop my interests in pastoral care and counselling with James Dittes and Russell Becker, and to take part in James Gustafson's postgraduate seminar on 'Christ and the Moral Life'. For me, this was a time of expanding horizons but still in the context of a more or less orthodox tradition of Western theology. James Dittes, while sympathetic to much of the modern counselling movement, warned against the 'seduction of relevance' which it posed for ministers. Russell Becker taught pastoral care from the perspective of a strong theological critique of Rogerian therapy and its implicit Doctrine of Man. James Gustafson introduced me to a range of reading in theological ethics. Alongside the academic stimulation, there was much more to take on board during that year. On Friday 22 November in the early afternoon, news came through of the assassination of President Kennedy, with all that followed. The civil-rights movement was at its height with fellow students setting out for the deep South on voter registration missions, often at risk to their lives. While those of us who were overseas scholars received strict instructions from the office of the World Council of Churches not to get involved, we could not but be part of the long and intense discussions which ensued about the social and political implications of the gospel.

I have had three very different experiences of ministry, first as a parish minister, then as a hospital chaplain and latterly as a university teacher of practical theology. My parish was in a new housing area on the Ayrshire coast. The congregation had been established for over 100 years, but five years previously had moved to a new building in the new housing area of the town. The Church of Scotland post-war church extension movement was at its height, 200 new buildings having been erected in 20 years. It was a time when congregations still grew if you did the right things. So we had a parish visitation and a stewardship campaign and I got out into the parish, and the numbers increased. Much time was spent on 'parish' funerals, ministering to families where there had been little previous contact with the Kirk, but I never felt this was time wasted. Most of my Kirk Session approved (though some did not) for we were a parish church, not simply a gathered congregation. Parish ministry was deeply satisfying, despite the odd elder who could not help being difficult. There was one who came to Kirk Session meetings clutching his own copy of Cox's *Practice and Procedure in the Church of Scotland* and sat there waiting to pounce – a difficult situation for a young minister to cope with. That was the kind of thing they did not teach you how to deal with in college.

After seven years I felt it was time to move on, and in 1971 I was appointed to a full-time hospital chaplaincy in Edinburgh. Part of the attraction of this post was a part-time appointment in the Faculty of Divinity, joining another two recently appointed full-time chaplains charged with developing supervised clinical placements for divinity students. Alastair Campbell was now teaching courses on pastoral care and counselling and on bioethics, subjects now fully integrated into the BD degree options and then being offered by a greatly expanded Department of Christian Ethics and Practical Theology, led by Professor James Blackie. For the next 15 years, I found the chaplaincy work itself was demanding and endlessly fascinating, as part of a chaplaincy team exercising pastoral care in a modern teaching hospital. There was a kidney transplant unit at one end and a department of neurosurgery at the other, as well as a large radiotherapy unit, general medicine and surgery, psychiatry and maternity. It was a period of rapid change. New technologies spawned new ethical dilemmas and these were never theoretical. Patients, their families and staff often found themselves involved in decisions which were quite literally matters of life and death. There was a ministry among staff as extensive as that among patients. Opportunities came to share in the teaching on pastoral and ethical issues in the College of Nursing. Chaplaincy itself was changing fast. It had to, because in the maelstrom of the modern hospital there was no place for the older style of chaplaincy: amateurish, detached and seemingly irrelevant. We had to become professional, but not so professional that we lost our role of being alongside people as ministers. For me it was important that in a teaching hospital, when virtually all the disciplines were involved in teaching and research, chaplaincy should do so also. Increasing numbers of divinity students were coming on courses and placements in all three hospital centres and a study of their changes in attitudes and skills provided ready data for research. It is not too much of an exaggeration to say that the bottom line of my PhD was an awareness that we taught divinity students how to say 'Mmm' rather than keep on asking interminable questions – a not inconsiderable achievement, and of great importance for their future ministry (Lyall 2000, 311ff).

In 1977, I received a phone call from Alastair Campbell which, in its consequences, would greatly enlarge my understanding of pastoral care. He was one of those instrumental in organizing the First International Congress on Pastoral Care and Counselling which was planned for Edinburgh in 1979. He asked if I would take on a major part of the administrative task which would be necessary in the run-up to the Congress. (When I asked 'Why me?' he muttered something about obsessive–compulsive tendencies.) The result of that initial work was a 20-year involvement in the work of the International Council on Pastoral Care and Counselling, much of it as its secretary. This has been an enormous privilege, meeting every two years in a different part of the world and engaging with those who in their own countries have been developing both the theory and practice of the ministry. My experience of the international pastoral care and counselling movement leads me to believe that in most countries the balance of activity is towards the pastoral care end of the spectrum. The exception is in the American pastoral counselling movement, where accreditation is mandatory for practice as a counsellor – and, incidentally, where ordination is a prerequisite for accreditation.

Since 1987 I have been teaching practical theology in two Scottish universities, first in St Andrews and since 1990 at Edinburgh as Alastair Campbell's successor after he left for a chair of bioethics in New Zealand. I teach courses on pastoral care and theology and some bioethics. I am essentially a practitioner who has landed up in academia, which I think (or at least hope) shapes the way I teach. I am also involved in organizing, and teaching in, a postgraduate Master's degree in ministry which over the past eight years has attracted, on a part-time basis, about 40 active ministers. Feedback indicates that they have benefited from reflecting upon their own pastoral ministry in an academic setting.

Why have I gone into my personal story in such detail? One reason is that it is integral to the nature of my argument in what follows. While I reject many of the conclusions which post-modernism is deemed to have for theology, I espouse enough to accept that much of our knowing is contextual and perspectival. I think it will become obvious that much of what I write comes out of my own history and context. In an article on 'Spiritual Autobiography', the American author Frederick Buechner (Kendrick 1992) is quoted as saying, 'My experience is that if anybody is willing to speak with some degree of candour – and with concreteness, that's the other important thing – then everyone is fascinated.' To invoke fascination might be too high an ambition, but I hope that in speaking concretely of my experience, I will give readers a better understanding of where I am coming from. As a minister of the Church of Scotland, I consider myself as coming from within the mainstream of a theological tradition which is reformed, catholic and ecumenical. I am neither a fundamentalist nor a radical. I am happy to affirm the Apostles' Creed Sunday by Sunday in the context of eucharistic worship.

Having had a long interest in pastoral care and counselling, I have to confess that I have never been accredited as a counsellor. I guess there are various possible reasons for this state of affairs. Perhaps it was lack of time (always a good excuse, for the time is never either ripe or available). Perhaps it was timidity and the fear of rejection. I think the real reason (though I admit the possibility of self-deception) is that I see myself as a minister and not as a counsellor. I have had various bits of counselling training over the past years. As well as the postgraduate year, there were three years of clinical theology while I was in the parish, and then a two-year-long psychoanalytic group and some clinical pastoral education in the United States, as well as other training experiences of various kinds. But I am not a counsellor, rather a minister who uses counselling skills as part of his ministry. I am encouraged by the fact that this 'confession' of mine, shared in conversation with some ministers for whose pastoral skills I have a high regard, seems to have brought an unexpected measure of relief. This is in no sense meant to be a disparagement of those ministers and lay people who feel a vocation to train as counsellors, pastoral or otherwise. It is merely to affirm that there is a ministry of pastoral care which, while incorporating many of the insights of good counselling, is not the same as counselling but which has its own integrity.

I have written what follows in the conviction that there is much good pastoral care being exercised in churches and communities by ministers (and lay people) who will never seek accreditation as counsellors. Hospital chaplaincy provides a unique vantage point from which to become aware of this. I have seen the committed and skilled work of visiting ministers at first hand. Patients describe in detail how their ministers have cared for them. One cannot but be humbled by their stories. The high quality of pastoral care being offered is confirmed for me by another source. A feature of the Edinburgh Master's degree in Ministry is reflection upon case material produced by participants. Some of this demonstrates deep commitment and perceptive ministry. As I began to write, I realized first of all that it was over ten years since I had been involved in active ministry – though work with students produces its own pastoral challenges. Second, I realized that there were readily to hand many examples of good pastoral practice which supported my argument. I therefore wrote to a number of colleagues, some of them former students, and asked them to share with me their experiences of ministry. These stories are incorporated in the text, and to those who have given of their time and themselves I express my deep appreciation.

The decision to ask fellow ministers to provide me with case material means that the ministries of counselling and pastoral care exercised by many lay people in churches and communities are under-represented in this book. This does not mean that I am unaware of their importance. Being married to someone who has been a Cruse bereavement counsellor and elder trainer, it could not be otherwise. I feel, however, that there is a need to reaffirm the contribution of the ordained ministry to the life of the Church, and that perhaps a dozen years' distance from front-line pastoral ministry sets me free to do this. In recent years the ordained ministry has had a bad press, the media making the most of those examples of ministerial frailty which come into the public domain. In most denominations there is also now a recognition that ministers are human beings who need the same kind of professional and personal support systems which are taken for granted in other professions. Paradoxically, however, the public recognition of this need has led to a focus on the need rather than on the fact that these needs are being met to the advantage of both ministers and congregations. Yet not all ministers are suffering from 'burn-out'; not all of them are depressed; not all of them are looking for alternative employment. I think the ministers who have supplied me with case material (as well as others) would use many words to describe their work. They would undoubtedly describe it as demanding, physically, emotionally and spiritually. They would certainly speak of it as challenging. But they would also want to affirm it as being deeply satisfying and worthwhile. I believe all of these words are implicit in the case studies, without which what I have written could not have been located in the realities of ministry. To those who have shared with me something of their work and of themselves, I dedicate this book, trusting that it may be both an affirmation and a celebration of the integrity of their ministry of pastoral care.

THE THESIS

My basic argument is that pastoral ministry has its own integrity rooted in the life and worship of the Christian Church, a community of faith which finds its identity in the events surrounding the story of Jesus of Nazareth. While pastoral ministry can gain much by drawing upon the insights of the human sciences and the secular psychotherapies, it is not at the end of the day dependent upon either their philosophies or their techniques. Pastoral care is not a poor relation of counselling, nor even a diluted form of pastoral counselling. Rather, pastoral care has its own history, theories, skills and theological basis.

TOWARDS A THEOLOGY AND PRACTICE OF PASTORAL MINISTRY . . .

In locating pastoral care within that story-formed community which is the Christian Church, one inevitably introduces an exploration of the relationship between theology and pastoral practice. How do the beliefs of the community of faith and of the individual pastor interact with the realities of the pastoral relationship? Is there a direct relationship between theology and pastoral practice? Or is the matter somewhat more complicated? I shall therefore introduce a discussion of different models which have tried to express the relationship between theology and pastoral care and advocate an understanding of the theology and practice of pastoral care which is shaped by the Christian narrative. This critical issue is set within the wider academic debate concerning the relationship between theology and practice, i.e. the contemporary debate about the nature of the discipline of practical theology itself.

. . . FOR POSTMODERN TIMES

It is with a degree of hesitation that I introduce the idea of postmodernism into this debate, largely because I lack the philosophical competence to deal with the issue adequately. I do so, however, for two reasons. First, the context of pastoral ministry is contemporary society and this has frequently been described as 'postmodern'. Various authors have begun to consider the nature of pastoral care in postmodern society including, in the United Kingdom, Goodliff (1999) and Hurding (1999) and in the United States, Patton (1994) and Fowler (1996). In a recent book, *Faithful Change: The Personal and Public Challenges of Postmodern Life* (1996), Fowler helpfully separates the concept of postmodern society, of 'practical postmodernism', from the abstract philosophical discussion of postmodernism. In that book, he is not primarily concerned with the practice of ministry, though I hope to show that his thinking has much relevance in this field. Fowler's focus is not upon abstruse academic theory but upon the ways in which people understand and describe their lived experience. The features of postmodernism which characterize that experience have variously been named as fragmentation, consumerism, globalization, religious pluralism, moral relativism and a communications revolution which is transforming the way we live and relate to one another. This is the contemporary context of pastoral ministry.

My second reason for introducing the concept of postmodernism is related to one of its central tenets and its implications for a theology and practice of pastoral ministry rooted in the Christian story. The French philosopher Jean-François Lyotard, in his book *The Postmodern Condition* (1984), argues that there is no longer any 'grand story' which can claim universal assent. Neither religion nor politics nor even science can provide any universal theory, any overarching belief system to which the majority of people can give their allegiance. A theology of pastoral care, therefore, which claims to be rooted in the Christian story must take seriously what has been called the 'postmodern critique of metanarrative'. If we wish to espouse a theology and practice of care which is funded by the Christian narrative we must at least consider the status of that story in the light of that critique.

THE IDEA OF INTEGRITY

Central to my argument is the belief that pastoral care has its own integrity. The word 'integrity' is itself complex and can be used in at least three senses. First, pastoral care has its own integrity as a form of ministry, and the nature of this 'professional' integrity is explored in the numerous case studies which permeate the book. Second, pastoral care has a theological integrity located within the biblical narrative. This is a statement which implies a particular understanding of the theology of pastoral care. For this reason an exploration of the current debate about the nature of pastoral theology and its relationship to wider issues within the related discipline of practical theology is a central theme. Third, pastoral care itself can provide a valuable integrating perspective on many aspects of the life of the Church. It is not the only lens through which one can view the worship and mission of the Church, but it is one which can bring into focus both the riches of the Christian tradition and the realities of the lived experience of the Church. This book does no more than touch upon this third use of the word, though much could be written about what happens when we look at worship, preaching, education, social action and mission through a pastoral lens. Our exploration, therefore, will focus particularly upon the first two of the above understandings of the nature of pastoral integrity, seeking to affirm pastoral ministry as having a professional integrity in itself and a theological integrity rooted in the Christian gospel.

CHAPTER ONE

Counselling, Pastoral Counselling, Pastoral Care and Ministry

THE ECLIPSE OF THE ORDAINED MINISTRY?

The particular focus of this book is the pastoral ministry exercised by those women and men in all branches of the Christian Church who have been ordained to the ministry of Word and sacrament. This proposal may require some justification in an age when other developments might seem to render it unfashionable or even anachronistic. Two such developments must be noted. First of all, there has been in all denominations a new (or renewed) emphasis upon the ministry of the laity, of the whole people of God. Second, there has been the phenomenal development of the secular psychotherapies and the modern counselling movement.

Looking first at what is happening within the churches themselves, we observe that ministry is no longer seen as belonging to 'the minister' alone. In liturgical renewal, lay people are finding their voice; in pastoral ministry, the gifts of the baptized are being discerned and liberated for care in congregations and communities. For 'the ordained' who have eyes to see and ears to hear, all this is cause for celebration. Theologically, the Church becomes more truly what it was meant to be; practically, the network of care is extended, no longer totally dependent upon the gifts and availability of time and energy on the part of the few. My purpose in this book is certainly not to play down the importance of the ministry of the whole people of God. Rather, it is to restore a sense of balance by reaffirming the contribution of the Church's traditional ministries of pastoral care to the healing and health of individuals and communities. This can be done on several grounds. First, the 'cure of souls' is at least as old as the Church itself, existing for nineteen hundred years before Sigmund Freud, the founder of psychoanalysis, uttered a thought. Historical studies by McNeill (1951) and by Clebsch and Jaekle (1964) can only draw attention to certain facets of a much larger phenomenon than can be recorded in textbooks. Throughout the Christian centuries there have been people with pastoral gifts exercised in the service of others. Prominent among the pastors of the Church have been its ordained ministers. Further, it is simply a fact that the churches still have a huge investment in their ordained ministries, though the pattern of the ordained ministry itself is changing. Most denominations rejoice in the special gifts which women are now able to bring to the ministry of Word and sacrament. New patterns of non-stipendiary or auxiliary ministry are setting free the gifts of others to be used in the service of the Church. Preparation for such ministries and on-going support in them have never been taken more seriously. The renewal of the whole people of God and a reaffirmation of the importance of the ordained ministry are not contradictory but complementary. True, new relationships must be worked out because the recovery of ordained ministry is not a reaffirmation of previous hierarchical structures. New challenges must be faced, new skills and attitudes developed 'to equip God's people for work in his service' (Ephesians 4.12 REB). In recent years there has been criticism, much of it justified, of the dominance of the 'clerical paradigm' (Farley 1983). What is required is not the rejection of such a paradigm but its reformation in the service of the Church. John de Gruchy, reflecting upon ministry from a South African perspective, writes:

> Clericalism is not overcome by rejecting an ordained ministry or by down-playing its significance and task. The church requires strong leadership both pastoral and theological, at all times but especially in a time of crisis. Edward Schillebeeckx, critical of clericalism as he is, points out that 'if there is no specialised concentration of what is important to everyone, in the long run the community suffers as a result'. All Christians, for example, are meant to be practical theologians, evangelists or priests, but some have a special calling, particular gifts, and are specially trained to fulfil such tasks within the body of Christ. In reflecting on the rediscovery of the ministry of the

laity within the ecumenical movement, Hans-Ruedi Weber once pertinently remarked: 'A high doctrine of the laity includes rather than excludes a high doctrine of the ordained ministry.' (de Gruchy 1987, 26)

Finally, it must also be recognized that there is much pastoral work of high calibre being done by ministers and others who will not seek accreditation as counsellors – and ought not to do so. While the Church and its ministers have much to learn from the secular therapies, ministers are generally not trained to function as such. I wish to deny neither the fundamental importance of the ministry of the whole Church nor the contribution of counselling to the healing of broken lives. At the same time, I argue that those set aside to exercise leadership in the church as ministers of Word and sacrament have a distinctive pastoral role, a role which is largely independent of confessional theologies of ordination. I believe that the various case studies which I will introduce throughout this book will demonstrate that this is indeed the case. I will argue that such pastoral care has its own integrity, and that a distinctive feature of such integrity is its deep roots within the Christian theological tradition. We cannot, however, ignore the impact of the modern counselling movement upon the pastoral role of the ordained ministry and upon public perceptions of that role.

THE COMING OF THE COUNSELLORS

'All of those involved in this terrible tragedy will be given counselling.' These words now seem to be a routine part of the media reporting of any event in which people have been severely traumatized. They point to one facet of the second development noted above, namely the remarkable growth of the modern counselling movement. There is much to be welcomed in this phenomenon. There is now a recognition that, in certain circumstances, men and women may need help to come to terms with traumatic events beyond their control. Those who become involved in such happenings in the course of their professional duties (such as the police and fire service), or members of the general public caught up in apparently random and appallingly tragic events such as took place in Dunblane in 1995, may benefit from the skilled help which a trained counsellor can bring to their individual distress. Two qualifications must, however, be made. There is now emerging a body of opinion which questions the value of the immediate debriefing of trauma victims. An article in *The Scotsman* (7 January 2000) is headed 'Counselling for victims of disasters "could be more hindrance than help"'. Referring specifically to the Dunblane situation, various psychologists are quoted, arguing that while some victims can benefit from skilled counselling after a period of time, many have not benefited from the immediate debriefing. It is asserted that a counsellor may in certain circumstances re-traumatize the person by regurgitating the most damaging experiences, and that sometimes a caring family member can help the individual by simply listening to their problems (Thompson 2000, 9). The second point worth noting is that while counsellors of every hue were queuing up to offer their services, it was Dunblane Cathedral, open to receive those who would come, that was to become the focus of the town's grief.

Nevertheless, generally speaking, there is now much greater and more explicit recognition of the contribution of counselling to specific human need and an implicit affirmation of the role of counselling in contemporary society. The last 30 or so years have witnessed a spectacular growth in counselling activity. To begin with, organizations were formed by concerned individuals in response to certain perceived needs. To mention only two of the better-known ones, the Marriage Guidance Councils were formed initially offering help to the increasing number of couples whose marriages were in trouble, and Cruse came into being to offer care and friendship to the bereaved. More recently, counselling courses have proliferated, offering diplomas and certificates. National organizations such as the British Association of Counselling have come into being, setting standards for what is effectively a new profession, and indeed there are many counsellors who have set up in private practice.

The expansion of counselling has had both positive and nega-tive aspects. On the one hand, standards have risen. Voluntary organizations, even those such as Cruse who continue to offer friendship, care and support, now require a professional standard of training from those who, on their behalf, offer what is described as 'counselling'. Further, the increasing prominence of counselling itself has made it more acceptable for troubled people to seek and accept help. No more need inner pain be borne with a stiff upper lip. On the other hand, amid all the good things that are happening, there are less positive aspects. First, the expansion of counselling has not necessarily been accompanied by an understanding of what counselling is all about. People cannot be 'given counselling' in the expectation that it is a kind of universal panacea for human distress. Counselling only 'works' (and even then not always) when those who enter counselling are able to make a commitment to the process, acknowledging their vulnerability and need of help. Again, the possession of a paper qualification in counselling does not guarantee that the holder is capable of forming the kind of human relationship which is essential in order to help another human being. While counselling courses proliferate, they vary in their quality, and those who call themselves counsellors have a wide range of training and experience as well as innate ability. Finally, there is a real danger that the increasing professionalism of care may de-skill those who have traditionally been involved in caring for others.

Despite these reservations, it must be recognized that the contribution of counselling and psychotherapy to human well-being has been significant and that the pastoral ministries of the Christian Church have themselves drawn to varying degrees upon their insights and practices. It is arguable that the impact of the modern counselling movement upon the ranks of the ordained ministry has been, at best, ambiguous. On the one hand, many have seen in the secular therapies new tools for ministry. There can be few ministers who are not aware of the importance of listening in a non-judgemental fashion to the stories told to them in the daily round of pastoral work. Some may indeed have had training in listening skills, and a significant minority have acquired enough training and experience in such approaches as Transactional Analysis or Clinical Theology for it to make a difference to their ministry. On the other hand, it is possible that the coming of the counsellors may have left many ministers among the ranks of the de-skilled, although this de-skilling may lie in the perception rather than in the reality. Certainly, ministers may perceive counsellors as having been trained, as having qualifications, and with a steady stream of clients coming to make use of their services, and accordingly they may see themselves as 'not being as good as' the counsellors. The reality may be somewhat different.

In speaking of the integrity of pastoral care, I wish to affirm the particular and peculiar contribution of ordained ministry to the health and healing of individuals and communities. Exercising a distinctive function within the Church and seldom in isolation from the community of faith, the ordained ministry is in a peculiar position to exercise a ministry of pastoral care in and on behalf of the Church. Drawing upon the insights and skills of the secular psychotherapies, such pastoral care finds its inspiration within biblical narrative rather than within their philosophies. Before launching into my substantive argument, however, a number of preliminary issues need to be addressed, and this I will attempt in the remainder of this chapter. These issues include:

- the nature and scope of pastoral care;
- pastoral counselling as a part of pastoral care;
- the meaning of the word 'integrity'.

THE NATURE AND SCOPE OF PASTORAL CARE

There are issues here relating to both definition and understanding. The use of the word 'pastoral' is now marked by complexity, if not confusion. The problem is partly one of definition. If one is looking for a definition of the word 'joule' then a perusal of half a dozen physics textbooks will provide only one answer (or, at least, six answers which are not mutually contradictory). Yet the search for a definition of the word 'pastoral' in several books on pastoral ministry may not provide the same degree of unanimity. Consider three recent definitions of pastoral care. For Alastair Campbell:

> Pastoral care is surprisingly simple. It has one fundamental aim: to help people know love, both as something to be received and as something to give. The summary of Jesus of all the Law and the Prophets in the two great Old Testament texts on love (Lev. 19.18 and Deut. 6.5) tells us . . . all we need to know about the tasks of Ministry. (Campbell 1985, 1)

Clebsch and Jaekle, the American authors of one of the classic histories of pastoral care, are much more specific in their definition:

> The ministry of the cure of souls, or pastoral care, consists of helping acts, done by *representative Christian persons*, directed towards the *healing, sustaining, guiding* and *reconciling* of *troubled persons*, whose troubles arise *in the context of ultimate meanings and concerns*. [authors' italics] (Clebsch and Jaekle 1964, 4)

Despite his reservations about this definition, not the least of these being its individualistic emphasis, Stephen Pattison sees in it enough value to offer for his own a development of this often quoted definition.

> Pastoral care is that activity, undertaken especially by representative Christian persons, directed towards the elimination and relief of sin and sorrow and the presentation of all people perfect in Christ to God. (Pattison 1988, 13)

As well as locating pastoral care quite specifically within the Christian tradition, this definition has several notable features. First of all Pattison is aware of the danger of describing pastoral care as an activity. In his *Rediscovering Pastoral Care* (1986), Alastair Campbell had stressed the importance of 'being' rather than of 'doing'. Nevertheless, Pattison wants to hold on to the idea that the purpose of pastoral care is to effect change. Second, the fact that pastoral care is undertaken 'especially' by representative persons holds in tension the recognition that it is not only ministers who engage in pastoral ministry, while at the same time recognizing the reality that much pastoral ministry is undertaken by those set aside by the Church specifically for this purpose. Third, the emphasis upon the aim to present *all* people perfect in Christ to God recognizes that the pastoral ministry can never be limited to card-carrying members of the Church. Finally, to speak of the 'elimination and relief of sorrow and sin' is to see the purpose of pastoral care as being far broader than simply supporting individuals in the context of their sorrows: it must also seek the transformation of the social and political situations which are the cause of human misery.

The problem is not simply one of definition but of perception. There are many people who have never read a book about pastoral care who yet have their own perspective on what they think pastoral care is or ought to be. In days gone by, there were clearer understandings of what pastoral care was all about. It was at least part of what ministers and priests were paid to do. They visited the sick and dying and comforted the bereaved. They even had time to visit their congregations systematically in their homes, getting to know families over a generation, becoming a respected – and sometimes loved – presence in the community. They were at the centre of community networks, the boundaries between congregation and parish or community being very permeable if they existed at all. It is perhaps possible that ministry in the past is viewed through rose-tinted spectacles. (Was it always true that a people-going minister created a church-going people?) There is little doubt, however, that faithfulness to the task, compassion for men and women and sometimes a deep insight into human nature achieved much of pastoral value. Nicolas Stacey, who eventually became Director of Social Work in a large London borough, writes of his time in parish ministry:

> It is difficult for priests to be dispassionate about the congregations committed to their care ... It is difficult not to love those whose secrets one knows and whose battles one helps to fight ... we coaxed them and cuddled them. We scolded them and sometimes swore at them, and laughed with them too. We prayed with them in private and did knees-up-Mother-Brown with them at parish socials in public. We visited them when they were sick and held their hands as they died. (Stacey 1971, 123–4)

There is no reason to doubt that this catches the flavour of the good pastoral ministry that characterized the 1960s, a time of theological ferment infused with a liberal optimism, a time which just antedated an approach to pastoral care which was beginning to be heavily influenced by the newly emerging psychotherapies. During the past 30 years or so, the situation has become more complicated. Various factors have combined to make the activity known as pastoral care a very complex phenomenon indeed.

First, it is now common practice for ministers-in-training to be given some training in human relationships and/or basic counselling skills. Theological colleges now spend a considerable time on the theory and practice of pastoral care, teaching approaches which to a greater or lesser degree are influenced by the secular therapies. It is to be hoped that ordinands go into their parishes or congregations with, for example, some theoretical understanding of the dynamics of grief or of the reality of transference and countertransference in pastoral relationships. Where these new insights are grafted on to innate pastoral gifts, ministry can only be enhanced. Where these gifts are lacking, however, the results can be questionable. 'At that point in the visit, I went into my counselling mode,' said one divinity student to me during a supervision session. 'She was in Kübler-Ross Stage Two,' said another.

Second, there is also a steady stream of ministers and priests seeking advanced training in counselling and they are – or can be – a significant and valued resource for the Church. Realizing the inevitably limited nature of the initial training received at theological college, they seek to develop their pastoral skills through long, personally demanding and usually expensive courses. The Church must learn to use such people. Being 'religious' is not a guarantee against becoming emotionally distressed, and there is not a little evidence that religion itself can be a factor in causing mental pain. What is sometimes needed is a counsellor who is both well trained as a counsellor and sensitive to the spiritual journey which is an integral part of what it means to be human. It is not, of course, only ministers and priests who are seeking advanced training in counselling. Increasing numbers of lay people, predominantly women, are also enrolling in courses and seeking qualification as counsellors. They too are a resource for the Church. Unfortunately, it is not every minister who is willing and able to use lay people with qualifications and competencies which far exceed their own. It is necessary to see how this highly specialized form of counselling, carried on within the context of the community of faith, relates both to the Church's broader ministry of pastoral care and to such counselling carried out in a purely secular context. To this we shall shortly turn.

Third, at a less intense but equally important level, lay people, as we have already noted, are assuming pastoral roles within congregations. Suitable women and men (and again it is mostly women) are being identified and trained to exercise an appropriate ministry as hospital visitors or in ministry to the shut-ins and elderly. On occasion, training is given to enable them to function as members of bereavement care teams, providing follow-up visits as the minister moves on to the new and ever-recurring crises. These teams are only effective and on-going where careful attention is given to the selection, training and continuing personal support of the visitors. My own limited observation is that it is those clergy who are most secure in themselves and in their own ministry who can make most effective use of lay visitors. Unfortunately there are still too many ministers who either need to have control or feel personally threatened by skilled lay people.

Fourth, there is a level of pastoral care, of people simply caring for one another, which just happens quite spontaneously. While the increased intentional training and use of lay people can only be welcomed, there is a danger of which we must be aware. People have always cared for one another, and that has been particularly true within Christian congregations. By identifying and empowering the few with special pastoral gifts we can end up de-skilling the many who just get on with it. I have a vivid recollection of three elderly widows in my congregation who sat together at the back of the church every Sunday and who provided on-going friendship for themselves and others. I remember the way they took another newly bereaved widow to themselves ('You are one of us now') and provided a quality of support which went far beyond what had been possible during the funeral and my own visiting. (They could easily have got this wrong but their intuitive action was in this case, I think, the right one.) Within churches and communities there are networks of care which bind people together and which enable them to live through the normal, and sometimes abnormal, crises of life. It would be tragic if someone felt that she could not visit a neighbour in need because she had not been on a course in listening skills.

Fifth, there must also be a recognition of the pastoral dimension of the care and counselling offered by Christians who work in what are generally regarded as secular counselling organizations. Within the ranks of those who counsel for Cruse and Relate (to mention only the ones which I know best) there are many who would identify themselves as Christians. For some it is expression enough of their faith that they offer a thoroughly professional counselling service in a secular setting, exercising a holy reticence in relation to what they themselves believe most deeply. What they are able to do is to respond sympathetically and without embarrassment to those parts of their clients' stories in which the spiritual pilgrimage is an important feature. What they will not attempt to do is to offer their own religious experience as providing a template within which clients' problems may be solved.

Finally, one further contemporary use of the word 'pastoral' must be considered, and that is one within education. In my own university, each student is allocated to a Director of Studies. Besides being responsible for helping each one of 50 or so students to chart their course through the complexity of degree regulations, each Director has an explicit 'pastoral' responsibility for each of his or her group of students, providing an interface with the university as an institution and a personal point of reference for any problems which may occur. The experience of the university is that Directors of Studies in all faculties play an invaluable role in providing support for students during what are often years of stress as well as challenge and enjoyment. Within schools, too, there is a recognition of the pastoral role of teachers. The National Association for Pastoral Care in Education has its own journal, *Pastoral Care in Education*, published by Blackwell. Past issues of the journal have dealt with topics such as 'bullying', 'working with a difficult class', 'preparing newly qualified teachers for a pastoral role', all pointing to a broad concern for an understanding of personal issues at the heart of the educational process. In neither of these two examples is there any religious overtone. It could be argued that this use of the word 'pastoral' is itself rooted in the Christian tradition, though it must be recognized that there are important understandings of pastoral care beyond the confines of the Church.

Thus, neither a study of the literature nor an observation of the practice of those who claim to exercise a ministry of pastoral care leads to a simple, commonly agreed understanding of the term. It is, however, incumbent upon someone who writes about pastoral care to make clear, even in the midst of confusion, his own understanding of the phenomenon about which he is writing! My next task, therefore, is to set down not a concise definition, but a statement of the parameters within which my own understanding of pastoral care falls. Then I will return to a fuller discussion of an issue raised above, namely the nature of pastoral counselling and its place within the wider pastoral ministry of the Church. It is pastoral care as set within these parameters which constitutes the pastoral paradigm which arguably has implications for other aspects of the life of the Church.

THE PASTORAL PARADIGM

Pastoral care is difficult to define because it is a phenomenon which is both simple and complex. Alastair Campbell is surely right when he points to its essential simplicity, with its one essential aim of helping people to know love, both as something to be received and something to give. Yet there is more to be said when it comes to working out what these definitions mean in practice. In the absence of generally agreed definitions all one can do is to make clear the boundaries of that understanding of pastoral care within which one is working. It is the delineation of these boundaries which, I think, constitutes the kind of pastoral paradigm assumed in this book and I set out its parameters in the following terms:

> Pastoral care involves the establishment of a relationship or relationships whose purpose may encompass support in a time of trouble and personal and/or spiritual growth through deeper understanding of oneself, others and/or God. Pastoral care will have at its heart the affirmation of meaning and worth of persons and will endeavour to strengthen their ability to respond creatively to whatever life brings.

> To name such care as 'pastoral' is to locate it within a community of faith, either because of its setting or because the carer is a designated representative of that community.

> Pastoral care is sensitive to the uniqueness of the spiritual journey of each human being, respecting the autonomy of individuals and their freedom to make their own choices.

> Pastoral care enjoys a freedom, but not a compulsion, to draw upon the traditional resources of the community of faith, such as prayer, Scripture and sacrament, the needs, stated or perceived, of the person receiving care being determinative.

> Pastoral care takes seriously the social and political context of care and its relationship to the total ministry of the Church, its ultimate aim being not merely adjustment to, but the transformation of, society.

> Pastoral care may take the form of a more intense pastoral counselling relationship which will respect both the recognized characteristics of good counselling and the above parameters of pastoral care.

This, then, is the understanding of pastoral care which is at the heart of what follows and in which the full implications of these parameters will be worked out. It does not encompass all the different understandings of pastoral care listed above. That is not to deny the importance of any of them in their own right, and it is particularly important to affirm the value of pastoral counselling as one aspect of the pastoral ministry of the Church.

PASTORAL COUNSELLING AS ONE FORM
OF PASTORAL CARE

To affirm that pastoral care rather than pastoral counselling is the normative pastoral ministry of the Church is not to devalue pastoral counselling as an important facet of that ministry. I have described elsewhere (Lyall 1993, 1995) the growth of counselling within the pastoral and spiritual context. Nevertheless, just as there are different understandings of the nature of pastoral care, so also are there different understandings of the nature of counselling within a Christian context. And, as we shall see, there are those who believe that to speak of counselling in a Christian context is a contradiction in terms.

There are counselling organizations which exist to make quite explicit the Christian understandings which inform their approach to counselling. Thus the rapidly growing Association of Christian Counsellors has a Statement of Faith which contains the following words:

> **Christian** counselling can be defined as 'that activity which seeks to help people towards constructive change and growth in any and every aspect of their lives. The aim is to achieve this through a caring relationship with agreed boundaries, **according to Biblical assumptions, aims and methods practised within a framework of Christian commitment, insight and values.**

This Statement of Faith, of which the words in bold letters are an integral part, makes quite explicit the theological parameters within which counselling takes place. Likewise the title of the Association of Biblical Counsellors locates its approach firmly within an explicitly Christian tradition. In a discourse in which words often carry more overtones of meaning than appears at face value, those who call themselves either Christian counsellors or biblical counsellors would generally take a more conservative, even fundamentalist, understanding of the Christian faith compared with those who would identify themselves as part of the pastoral counselling movement.

Whatever the subtleties of difference in theological flavour between Christians involved in counselling it has also to be recognized that there are those who have no taste for any kind of counselling rooted in the Christian tradition. In an interesting review of a previous book of mine, Julia Buckroyd (1996) writes:

Counselling is dedicated to increasing the autonomy of the individual and in providing the environment in which individuals can find their own answers to their own questions. The Christian religion on the other hand is based on the idea that it possesses knowledge and truth which have been revealed by God. The Christian Church professes to know what is right behaviour in a significant number of situations, notably in the area of human sexual behaviour. Since this area is one which impinges upon virtually all human beings, and certainly many of those seeking counselling, I do not understand how a pastoral counsellor can be encouraging autonomy in a client when he or she already knows the 'right answer' to a dilemma presented to him or her. How for example can a Catholic priest 'counsel' on the matter of abortion? Encourage, support, instruct, yes: counsel, no.

Ms Buckroyd is undoubtedly raising important issues, and to some extent we must recognize that she offers a valid criticism of the manner in which the Church has sometimes responded to issues of human sexuality. Yet her blanket condemnation is perhaps somewhat 'over the top'. For one thing, not all Christian pastors would claim 'to know what is right behaviour in a significant number of situations'. Indeed, the charge which is often laid against the present-day Church, particularly its liberal wing, is precisely that it does not know what it believes and that it fails to give a moral lead, especially in the area of human sexuality. The fact is that there are many pastoral counsellors who would not approach their task believing that either abortion or homosexual practices were wrong in themselves. It must be questioned, however, whether it is not a little naïve to imagine that counselling is a totally value-free activity designed to increase the autonomy of individuals and to encourage them to find their own answers to their own questions. Does this philosophy apply to the counselling of men who have sexually abused children or done violence to women? While there will surely be the provision of an accepting relationship in which the causes of such unacceptable behaviour may be understood, can any counselling take place except on the basis that certain behaviours are wrong and must stop? Value-free counselling is a myth. What is important is that those who counsel are aware of the values which they themselves bring to their counselling and the way in which these values affect their practice.

What then is pastoral counselling? Is it really *counselling*? How does it differ from the various kinds of secular counselling? And is it different from the more explicitly Christian approaches to counselling? In line with my attempt to set the boundaries of my own understanding of pastoral care, I offer the following propositions which I believe must characterize any activity which describes itself as pastoral counselling. Inevitably there is some overlap with the more general activity of pastoral care.

First, pastoral counselling is a form of counselling. It is grounded in some coherent theory and, with the best of the secular approaches, it shares a commitment to a high standard of experience-based learning supported by competent supervision. Pastoral counselling is not, of course, a single thing and there are various models of pastoral counselling, many of which draw upon the insights of one or more of the secular psychotherapies. There are pastoral counsellors whose understanding of human growth and development is largely shaped either by the psycho-dynamic or Jungian or person-centred approaches, to mention only three. Each of the secular therapies has contained within it implicit assumptions about what it means to be human. What the pastoral counsellors must not do is to fall into an uncritical acceptance of such assumptions; rather, they must bring to them a critique based upon a Christian understanding of what it means to be human. This is not a simple process and constitutes one of the main issues in pastoral theology to which I will return in a later chapter.

Second, pastoral counselling is comfortable with human religious experience. For many the spiritual journey is part of what it means to be human, though this may be expressed neither in credal conformity nor in regular church-going. While secular counsellors can be embarrassed by religion and Christian counsellors can be obsessed with it, pastoral counsellors can celebrate it as a source of meaning and a resource for living. From this, several things follow. Clearly professional integrity demands that a counsellor refrain from imposing his or her own meanings upon the client. Nevertheless, where there are shared meanings there need be little hesitation about exploring these as part of the counselling process. It might, for example, be entirely appropriate for there to be some exploration of issues related to the client's understanding of death and resurrection in the pastoral counselling of someone who has been bereaved.

This does not mean to say that all manifestations of religion are equally helpful. There are varieties of religion which enslave and expressions of faith which liberate; there is sick religion and there is healthy religion. It is here that the psychologists of religion have an important contribution to make, though it should not be forgotten that theologians such as Barth and Bonhoeffer have also had something to say about the pathological nature of religion as such. Freud has been rightly criticized on the grounds that his somewhat negative view of religion has been based upon his encounters with clients whose religiosity was integral to their pathology. Nevertheless, he did expose some of the ways in which religion functioned in an unhealthy way in some people's lives. William James in his famous Gifford Lectures of 1900 made a clear distinction between 'healthy-mindedness' and X the 'sick soul' and indeed affirmed that religion itself had a crucial role in the promotion of the former:

> Repentance according to such healthy-minded Christians means *getting away from* the sin, not groaning and writhing over its commission. The Catholic practice of confession and absolution is in one of its aspects little more than a systematic method of keeping healthy-mindedness on top. (James 1900, 138)

Eric Fromm in *Psychoanalysis and Religion* (1950) makes a clear distinction between *authoritarian* and *humanistic* religions, noting that the former can find secular as well as what are normally considered to be religious expressions (e.g. the worship of the Führer in Nazi Germany). Authoritarian religion enslaves and induces guilt and the fear of punishment. Humanistic religion, on the contrary,

> is centred around man and his strength. Man must develop his power of reason in order to understand himself, his relationship to his fellow men and his position in the universe. He must recognize the truth both with regard to his limitations and his possibilities. He must develop his powers of love for others as well as for himself . . . Faith is certainty of conviction based upon one's experience of thought and feeling, not assent to propositions on credit of the proposer. The prevailing mood is that of joy, while the prevailing mood in authoritarian religion is that of sorrow and guilt. (Fromm 1950, 37)

The task of the pastoral counsellor is to explore how religion functions in a client's life and, where religion appears to be dysfunctional, to help the client use the resources of his faith more creatively. There is, of course, a value judgement, or at least a clinical one, on the part of the counsellor as to what constitutes dysfunctional religion and this is true for the pastoral as much as for the secular counsellor. There is also the possibility that the pastoral counsellor will be better equipped to make such a differential diagnosis. Over-attachment to a liberal *zeitgeist* may not liberate the personality; deep commitment to a well-considered orthodoxy need not enslave it.

Third, pastoral counselling takes seriously social and political context. There are two senses in which this is so. As often as not, the primary context of pastoral counselling is some expression of the Christian community, be it a local congregation or chaplaincy or church-related counselling centre. There are, certainly within the United Kingdom, very few independent counsellors who describe themselves as 'pastoral counsellors'. This does not mean to say that there are not many counsellors who are deeply committed Christians – this has already been alluded to. The point is that those who describe themselves as 'pastoral counsellors' tend to work in the context of a community of faith. Further, to describe oneself as a pastoral counsellor is to lay oneself open to being on the receiving end of all the religious projections, both positive and negative, which clients inevitably bring to the pastoral relationship. Those who call themselves pastoral counsellors must be aware of the perceptions and expectations, justified or not, which such a self-description may invoke.

There is, however, another aspect to the social and political context of pastoral care. If pastoral counsellors must have an awareness of the communal dimension of their own context, neither can they ignore the social and political context of their clients. Much of the pastoral counselling of a previous generation, mirroring the ethos of the contemporary secular counselling, can be criticized for its focus upon the individual self-realization in isolation from any wider context. It has been the particular genius of those responsible for the development of pastoral studies in the University of Birmingham to explore the necessary relationship between pastoral care and political context. Robert Lambourne (1974), Michael Wilson (1985) and, following after them, Stephen Pattison (1997) and Emmanuel Lartey (1997) have all pointed to the danger of a pastoral practice which is individualistic, medicalized, psychotherapeutically oriented and apolitical. More recent writing, for example the collection of papers edited by Pamela Couture and Rodney Hunter (1995), has pointed to the need to consider the matrix of social interaction

and conflict which provides the context in which pastoral relationships are established and the limits within which personal
and spiritual growth must take place. This last publication is of
particular interest, coming as it does from North America, where
for the past 50 years pastoral care has been dominated by secular
psychotherapeutic models which were largely individualistic.

Fourth, pastoral counselling has at its core a set of theological
convictions, whether explicit or implicit. I have suggested above
that there is no such thing as value-free counselling. I wish to go
further and to claim that within those activities which describe
themselves as either pastoral care or pastoral counselling, there
are assumptions of a theological nature which are integral to
them. The central issue in the discipline known as pastoral
theology is the relationship between theological understanding
and pastoral practice, whether through pastoral care, or more
specialized forms of pastoral counselling, or through any other
aspect of the ministry of the Church which has a pastoral dimension. Indeed, it is arguable that many aspects of the life of the
Church could be viewed through a pastoral lens. It could be
demonstrated that a pastoral paradigm can throw light on the
nature of preaching and worship, upon ethical decision-making
and social action, as well as upon what is sometimes understood
more narrowly as the pastoral tasks of the Church. Thus, while
this book is predominantly about pastoral care, it is in no sense
a rejection of the need for highly trained and qualified pastoral
counsellors who, probably more often than not, will offer their
services within the context of the community of faith.

My aim in this book is not to discount the contribution of
well-trained counsellors to contemporary society, and indeed it
goes without saying that good counselling, appropriately used
and whether 'secular' or 'pastoral', has made an immense contribution to human well-being. Within the context of my argument,
pastoral counselling is one expression of pastoral care, and a
crucially important one at that. Pastoral care and pastoral counselling are integrally related to one another. But if they cannot be
separated from one another, neither can they be identified with
one another.

THE INTEGRITY OF PASTORAL CARE

Having set out my understanding of the nature of pastoral
care, what do I mean when I speak of its 'integrity'? In his

Rediscovering Pastoral Care, Alastair Campbell has highlighted two aspects of integrity, both of which are related to the personality and being of the carer. The first he describes as 'Honesty and Steadfastness'.

> To possess integrity is to have a kind of inner strength which prevents us from bending to what is thought expedient, or fashionable, or calculated to win praise; it is to be consistent and trustworthy because of a constancy of purpose. Yet the honesty conveyed by the word integrity must not be confused with inflexibility and dogmatism, with the refusal to recognise error in oneself and in the inability to perceive and respond to change in things around one. (Campbell 1986, 12)

Second, Campbell sees such integrity based on 'Wholeness and Oneness', the ability of the carer to 'retain or to regain contact with the lost and repudiated aspects of ourselves' (Campbell 1986, 14). In Jungian terms, it is to be in touch with the mysterious centre of our being, hard to describe or discuss, yet indispensable to our integrity. It is at the centre of our being that we encounter transcendence, summed up in the words of Thomas Merton as he seeks to explain the meaning of the concept of 'the heart' in traditional writings on prayer:

> It refers to the deepest psychological ground of one's personality, the inner sanctuary where self-awareness goes beyond analytical reflection, and opens out into metaphysical and theological confrontation with the Abyss of the unknown yet present – one who is 'more intimate to us than we are to ourselves'. (Campbell 1986, 15)

For Campbell, pastoral care consists essentially in 'the mediation of steadfastness and wholeness, not the offering of advice at an intellectual level, nor the eliciting of insight at an emotional level'. It involves an understanding of integrity as closely related to a concept of spirituality, encompassing a vision both of authentic humanity and genuine transcendence. The humanity is authentic because it takes seriously both the realities and the possibilities of human existence. The transcendence is genuine because it points in a non-dogmatic way to the experience of the Other at the heart of life.

In setting out my own understanding of the integrity of pastoral care, I do not wish to detract from Campbell's moving and poetic reflections on pastoral integrity. His comments refer to the integrity of the pastor. There are, however, three more prosaic comments which I wish to make, concerning not so much the integrity of the pastoral agent as the nature of the pastoral task itself. These relate to:

1 The integrity of pastoral care as a discipline.
2 The theological integrity of pastoral care.
3 Pastoral care as an integrating paradigm.

1 THE INTEGRITY OF PASTORAL CARE AS A DISCIPLINE

To speak of the integrity of pastoral care is to point to the fact that it is a discipline in its own right. It is neither a 'Mickey Mouse' form of counselling nor amateur social work. Grounded historically in the worship and life of the Church, at its best it has exercised a profound caring ministry for men and women in the midst of their communities. Indeed, in *The Faith of the Counsellors* (1965), Paul Halmos traces the roots of the modern caring professions back to the philosophies of faith and love which have been at the heart of the ministries of the Church. While pastoral care has its own integrity, it is not isolationist. Pastoral care is essentially interdisciplinary in nature. As we have noted, it has felt free to draw upon the insights of the counselling movement and to baptize them in the service of pastoral ministry. Further, with their myriad of day-to-day contacts with people in communities, it may well be pastors who develop a sense that all is not well with an individual or family and encourage them to seek help which lies beyond their pastoral competence. Referral is a pastoral art, knowing how and when to refer – and when not to do so.

2 THE THEOLOGICAL INTEGRITY OF PASTORAL CARE

I have located pastoral care as taking place within communities of faith. Such communities are not random collections of individuals. They are shaped by historical traditions, credal statements and confessions, modes of worship, ethical codes. This does not mean that all who identify with communities of faith are identical in their faith and practice. There is room for diversity and even disagreement. Yet every faith community is shaped by its own story and the way in which that story has been interpreted and passed on as generation has succeeded generation.

The fundamental narrative of the Christian Church is the story of God's self-revelation in Jesus Christ, as witnessed to in the Scriptures of the Old and New Testaments. These stories have been interpreted afresh in every generation, shedding light on the current practice of the faith community. Pastoral theology is concerned with the relationship between theology and pastoral practice. Therefore, part of this work will be devoted to a consideration of recent and present debates about how contemporary pastoral care is shaped by, and can find its own integrity or inner cohesion within, the Christian story. A characteristic of the present time, sometimes known as 'postmodernity', is that stories such as the Christian story do not enjoy the widespread acceptance that they once did. It will be necessary, therefore, to examine how far the postmodern critique of the Christian story detracts from its ability to shape pastoral care within the Christian community.

3 PASTORAL CARE AS AN INTEGRATING PARADIGM

While arguing for an intimate relationship between belief and practice, we must also note that such a relationship is not unidirectional. While practice is undoubtedly shaped by belief, it is also arguable that pastoral practice itself can help us to understand more fully other aspects of the life and work of the Church. The 'pastoral paradigm' can have an integrative function in relation to much of the life of the Church. A pastoral care which finds its identity rooted in biblical narrative provides a rich paradigm for understanding and interpreting other aspects central to the life of the Christian Church. These include the sacramental life of the Church and the proclamation of grace which is at the heart of Christian worship. While it lies beyond the scope of this book, it would not be difficult to demonstrate that the pastoral paradigm has illuminative and integrative power as it is brought to bear upon the different aspects of the Church's being in the world.

We turn now to a consideration of the relationship between theology and practice, arguably the central issue in the theology of pastoral care and in the recently rediscovered discipline of practical theology.

CHAPTER TWO

Theology and Pastoral Practice

THE CASE OF THE INARTICULATE ORDINAND

A mature ordinand came on a hospital placement towards the end of his course. He was an able man who had decided to 'train properly' for the ministry. He had therefore acquired a good degree in philosophy and was nearing the completion of a Bachelor of Divinity course specializing in Systematic Theology. After the usual orientation to working as a member of the chaplaincy team, he set out to visit patients on one of the surgical wards. Half an hour later he returned to the Chaplaincy Centre in a somewhat distraught state. Over a cup of coffee he calmed down and revealed the source of his distress. It was not simply the intensity of human suffering, both physical and emotional, which he had encountered as he moved from one patient to another, though in all truth there was plenty of that around. No, the problem for him was much more fundamental. 'When I met these people, I had nothing to say,' he confessed. 'What has all this study been for? Four years of philosophy and three years of dogmatics and when I encounter real people I don't have a word for them. I have been wasting my time!'

How did it come about that a man who knew so much had nothing to say? How was it that someone who had thought so deeply about the meaning of suffering from philosophical and theological perspectives was struck dumb in the face of the reality of suffering? The answers to these questions are complex.

Indeed, some might find it a sign of grace that he did not rush into speaking for the sake of speaking. Or the inarticulateness in this case may be peculiar to the man. It may well be that he was the kind of person who did not wish to listen, indeed simply *could not* listen, to the deep pain of another human being. Or he may have been someone who had to be in control of every situation or to be a 'problem solver'. Quite apart from such psychological speculation, however, this incident also raises fundamental issues relating to method in practical and pastoral theology. Before returning to a fuller exploration of the above case we shall examine two very different models for relating theology and pastoral practice.

What is the relationship between our beliefs and our practice? How does our understanding of the faith affect what we do in our pastoral relationships? Is there any such connection and, indeed, should there be? Very different answers have been given to these questions. At one extreme there are Christian counsellors who conceive their task in terms of the direct application of their Christian beliefs to every human situation; at the other end of the spectrum, there are secular counsellors, and indeed some pastoral ones, who hold that the beliefs of the counsellor must be totally 'bracketed out' from the counselling process; I shall attempt to expose the inadequacies of both of these extreme positions while at the same time arguing for a relationship between theology and pastoral practice which takes seriously biblical narrative. Before constructive work can begin, however, it is necessary to clear the ground, to dig deep into the foundations which have already been laid and to see if these are adequate.

DEFINITIONS

First of all, a word about definitions. It has to be recognized that some terms have been used in different ways in different parts of the Christian Church. For example, the term *pastoral theology* has, largely in Catholic circles, sometimes been an umbrella term to describe that discipline concerned with all the practical work of the priest. Within Protestantism, the term *practical theology* has served the same kind of function with regard to its own ordained ministry. During my own period of theological education in the early 1960s, 'PT' was a practical discipline providing instruction on how to lead worship and conduct baptisms, weddings and funerals (and how not to become too deeply involved with parishioners). Practical theology, certainly within the Reformed tradition, was a term used to describe the study of all the functions of the ordained ministry.

Within the past 20 years, a sea-change has taken place in the discipline. A consideration of practice alone has been transformed into a branch of theology which explores the relationship between theology and practice. Theology is here understood as critical and faithful reflection upon the Scriptures and tradition of the Church; 'practice' refers to the whole life of the Church, its worship and pastoral care, its ethical reflection and social and political engagement with the world in which it finds its life and mission. We should note that nowadays it is more common to speak of praxis than practice. The word 'praxis', with its roots in recent liberation theology, bears witness to the perception that there is no such thing as 'mere practice' without an ideological hinterland and that all practice originates from a worldview which is the healthier for being made open and explicit rather than remaining covert and implicit. More will be said later about the contemporary debate in practical theology. For the time being, it is sufficient to note the current understanding of practical theology as that branch of theology which is concerned to explore the relationship between, on the one hand, Scripture and the tradition of the Church and, on the other hand, the whole range of Christian praxis in the world. Pastoral theology then becomes that branch of practical theology specifically concerned with the interaction between theology and that part of Christian praxis denoted by the term 'pastoral care'. Thus current debate about the nature of practical theology is integral to any understanding of the theology of pastoral care. That debate has its roots within nineteenth-century theological exploration.

FRIEDRICH SCHLEIERMACHER AND THE ROOTS OF PRACTICAL THEOLOGY

The first to outline critically the concept of 'practical theology' was Friedrich Schleiermacher, the leading German theologian of the nineteenth century. Farley (1990, 934) shows how the late eighteenth century, influenced by the rationalism of the Enlightenment, had seen the systematization of theological studies in German universities, with biblical, philosophical and practical theology together with church history emerging as the four standard theological disciplines. Schleiermacher, however, in his *Brief Outline of the Study of Theology* (1811/1830) divided theology into three parts – historical, philosophical and practical – with a particular relationship between them. It was practical theology which was 'the crown of theological study' because his whole theological method was designed to lead up to practical theology as the application of theology to the service of the Church. Schleiermacher brought order into the whole field of practical theology. Further, he was insistent that church leadership was primarily about the cure of souls. There is, however, a fundamental problem arising from his theological method which has exercised a continuing and formative influence. This follows as a direct consequence of his premise that the relationship between philosophical theology and practical theology is in one direction only, which he states as follows:

> The two (philosophical theology and practical theology) stand over against each other, partly in relation of the first to the last, since it is philosophical theology that first fixes the subject matter with which practical theology has to deal, and partly in that philosophical theology fastens upon certain purely scientific constructions while practical theology, *in its role as technology* [italics mine], is largely attached to the individual and the particular. (Schleiermacher 1830, 29)

Thus it is philosophical theology (of which dogmatic theology is a part) which determines the practice of ministry. Practical theology, in its role as 'technology', cannot by definition have any input to the corpus of theological knowledge. This understanding of practical theology, practical theology as 'applied theology', has been dominant in Protestant theological thought right to the middle of the twentieth century, that is until the advent of the recent new explorations into the nature of the discipline which I mentioned above. We find its fullest expression in the pastoral theology of Eduard Thurneysen, heavily influenced by the neo-orthodox theology of his colleague and friend Karl Barth.

PASTORAL CARE AS APPLIED THEOLOGY

Thurneysen, like many in bygone days who found their vocation in the theological academy, had experience of the realities of pastoral ministry, being pastor of the Munster in Basel before becoming Professor of Practical Theology at the university in that city. His book, *A Theology of Pastoral Care* (1962), has been a definitive and influential statement of a neo-orthodox approach to pastoral theology.

For Thurneysen, pastoral care exists in the Church as the communication of the Word of God to individuals. Pastoral care does not take the place of sermon and sacrament but accompanies them. Pastoral care is integral to the discipline of the Church.

> Since God will not abandon the individual, pastoral care is a means of leading him to sermon and sacrament, and thus to the Word of God, of incorporating him into the Christian community and of preserving him in it. So understood, it is an act of sanctification and of discipline by which the visible form of the community is constituted and kept alive, and by which the individual is redeemed and preserved in spite of his degeneration and corruption. (Thurneysen 1962, 32)

It is this theological perspective which protects pastoral care from being confused with the nurture of souls carried on by means of modern psychology. Pastoral care is care for the soul of man, but man's soul is not simply his psychic element: rather, it is the totality of his existence under God. Pastoral care is essentially care grounded in the Word of God, in which man's natural articulation is put in the service of the Holy Spirit. It is here that Thurneysen breaks decisively with Schleiermacher, according to whom man's salvation depends upon the natural articulateness of the preacher and therefore, by extension into pastoral care, upon the psychological competence of the pastor. For Thurneysen, good Barthian that he is, this is anathema. Because pastoral care is grounded in the Word of God and because it depends ultimately neither on man's innate capacity for God nor upon the technical competence of the pastor, then there must be what he calls 'a breach in the pastoral conversation'. This means that while 'hardly any pastoral conversation can be conducted without psychology being applied', psychology does not have the last word. That belongs to the Word of God, though this does not mean that genuine listening can be dispensed with. But what is the content of this pastoral conversation?

> Like the proclamation of the church generally, pastoral conversation has as its only content the forgiveness of sins in Jesus Christ ... man in his totality is addressed as a sinner under grace. (Thurneysen 1962, 147)

The forgiveness of sins signifies the coming into force of a peace treaty which God has concluded with men in Jesus Christ. Sinful man has waged a conflict with God, but forgiveness is the peace whereby God terminates this conflict. This peace is not simply 'peace of mind', but the peace of God which is beyond human understanding.

Despite his view that psychology made no contribution to our theological understanding of man as created by God and redeemed by Christ, Thurneysen did see a positive role for both psychology and psychotherapy in the relief of human distress. Psychology is the science devoted to the exploration of the inner life of man; psychotherapy is the chief form in which psychology is applied to emotional disturbances and illnesses. Pastoral care, however, is not identical with either psychotherapy or psychiatry, though psychological understanding of man may prepare the way for the proclamation of grace and forgiveness. Since 'according to the Word of God, man's natural sickness is to be understood as a symptom indicative of a much deeper, meta-physical disturbance', pastoral care is concerned with allowing man to see himself in the light of his sin and God's forgiveness, 'to examine the natural event of illness and healing in the light of faith' (Thurneysen 1962, 225).

Thurneysen believes that psychology is a purely phenomeno-logical science and that the psychologist can make no metaphysical speculation about the nature of man. As there is no Christian physics, so also is there no Christian psychology. Psychology can say nothing about the mystery of man's humanity before God; this is the exclusive content of the biblical understanding of man. 'Sin' and 'grace' do not belong to the vocabulary of psy-chology, but pastoral care stands or falls by the biblical view of man as a sinner under grace. What happens when a pastor neglects this biblical view and tries to understand him other-wise, i.e. in terms of psychological and natural presuppositions? Then, argues Thurneysen, the task of pastoral care is betrayed:

He will no longer use psychology as a necessary auxiliary science; rather he will begin to practice pastoral care as an auxiliary to the norm of psychology . . . Pastoral care then becomes psychological counsel in religious garb. (Thurneysen 1962, 214)

We see, therefore, that Thurneysen's approach was essentially one of applying the certainties of gospel truth to the realities of the human situation. It was based upon a theology of proclamation and the conviction that in the Word of God alone there was balm sufficient to relieve human sin and sorrow. There were inevitable consequences for pastoral education.

'APPLIED THEOLOGY' AND LEARNING TO CARE

Let us now return to the story of the ordinand with which this chapter began. In subsequent supervision sessions, several issues were addressed, most of which need not concern us here. Among them, however, was his understanding of the nature of theology and how he thought his theology ought to influence his practice. Before he began his placement, he thought, rather naïvely as it turned out, that the 'book answers', whether from the Bible or from theological texts, would be sufficient in themselves. Their insufficiency became for him what the literature of pastoral supervision calls 'a critical incident' (Foskett and Lyall 1988, 74) in his growth as a minister. He came to see that his inarticulateness in that situation was a sign of grace, that knowing that one does not enter into pastoral situations with a ready 'word' for everyone is the start of becoming a good pastor. This is not to decry the importance of a sound theology as a foundation ministry – would that all students took their academic preparation as seriously as this man did – because, as we shall see, we need to have an approach to pastoral care of which the gospel is an integral part. The issue, however, is not that of *applying* but of *relating* the Christian story to our pastoral practice.

Supposing, however, that this student had persisted in his belief that academic study should have provided him with a suitable word for every occasion. Underlying this position there is an assumption about the nature of theology. That assumption is that theology is essentially propositional and is learned from lectures or found in books in libraries. And if in any given situation one does not have the 'right' theological answer, then the only recourse is return to the place where the answers are to be found, namely the books, where surely someone will have something relevant to offer. But then the theology being applied is someone else's theology. In a paper on 'Educational Models in Field Education', James and Evelyn Whitehead pinpoint the problems with this approach to learning about ministry:

> In the application of theory model the assumption is, as we
> have seen, that theological learning occurs in the classroom

and is then practically applied in field education. The ministerial student is invited to see himself as an administrator, a
communicator of the tradition, and in the worst realization of
the model, as a functionary. The student can easily understand
his role as applying what theologians have reflected upon and
decided. His ministry does not include his own theologizing,
but rather his application of someone else's theologizing to his
own specific ministerial situation . . . The peculiarity of this
model is that the student is encouraged to recognize himself
as a nontheologian. His application of theory then becomes
a one-directional activity since his location of the theological
enterprise disallows his theological questioning of the tradition. (Whitehead and Whitehead 1975, 272)

And, we might add, it is the unsuccessful attempt to apply someone else's theology – which is inevitably a propositional theology
– to the realities of the pastoral situation which leads, for the
pastoral practitioner, to the separation of theology and practice.

Having examined one attempt to construct a theology of pastoral care heavily dominated by the paradigms of academic
theology we now turn to another approach with its roots in a
very different cultural milieu.

PASTORAL CARE AS APPLIED PSYCHOLOGY

From a theology of pastoral care rooted in the neo-orthodox
theology of post-war continental Europe we turn to another
understanding of the nature of pastoral theology, one which
owes much to the psychological orthodoxies of mid-twentieth-
century North America. I have outlined elsewhere the American
contribution to the development of pastoral care and counselling
(Lyall 1995). The 20 years after the Second World War witnessed
the phenomenal growth of new secular psychotherapies. The
contribution of Carl Rogers and his *Client-Centered Therapy* (1951)
to pastoral care and counselling is now well recognized, and
Allison Stokes in her *Ministry After Freud* (1985) has documented
the concurrent impact of Freudian theory upon pastoral ministry. At that time, the mainstream of North American theological
opinion was predominantly liberal. This is not surprising, especially when we view the rise of neo-orthodox theology in the
context of the European response to the totalitarian regimes of
that period. Thurneysen's pastoral care and theology can be

understood as a function of a church seeking to be distinctive in the midst of the surrounding cultural and political pressures. In contrast, North American pastoral care (and what pastoral theology there was) found it easy to accommodate itself to the insights and philosophies of these newer therapies which both reflected and contributed to the prevailing culture of optimism and self-realization. With its heavy dominance upon the secular therapies, the main focus in pastoral education shifted to the acquisition of counselling and relational skills which could be utilized in ministry. However, as the Whiteheads pointed out in the above article, this approach to pastoral education was not without its negative consequences.

> When the ministerial student learns counselling skills, he most often does so in an extra-theological context. Since the vocabulary and rhetoric he learns are those of another profession, the student is often left with the question: how am I different from a non-ministerial counsellor? One acutely negative result of such a bifurcation of theological and pastoral education can be that the student recognises he is neither a theologian (his teachers have probably made that clear), nor a professional counsellor . . . The common result of such an approach is that the ministerial student either tries to adjust to an image of himself as an inadequate theologian or an inadequate counsellor, or he obtains competency in his pastoral skill, and then leaves the ministry to pursue the professional practice of his skill. (Whitehead and Whitehead 1975, 275)

Thus if the 'applied theology' model leads to a divorce between theology and practice, in the 'applied psychology' model, based upon the acquisition of counselling skills, there can be no talk of separation because theology and practice have never been introduced to one another, let alone been in the same bed.

Several books on pastoral counselling were written during this period when the whole counselling movement was blossoming in North America, and reading books such as Carroll Wise's *Pastoral Counseling: Its Theory and Practice* (1951) and Seward Hiltner's *Pastoral Counseling* (1949) helps one capture the sense of excitement and freedom which permeated the exploration of this new resource for ministry. Yet neither of these made any real attempt to engage in much theological reflection. Both were prepared to draw upon 'religious resources', yet these were not central but rather an optional, sometimes useful, tool to their approach to counselling which was essentially secular in both its philosophy and practice (Wise 1951, 145). It is this phase of the modern pastoral movement which I think can fairly be categorized as 'applied psychology'.

PASTORAL THEOLOGY AND THE PRINCIPLE OF CORRELATION

Over the next decades, Hiltner became increasingly aware of the theological barrenness which afflicted much of the current pastoral care and counselling movement. In two subsequent books, he attempted to establish a pastoral theological method which made connections with the traditional theological disciplines without denying the enormous gains in pastoral skills achieved through interaction with the secular psychotherapies. Of major importance is his *Preface to Pastoral Theology* (1958) in which he sets forth and elaborates his thesis that

> Pastoral theology is a field of theological knowledge and inquiry that brings the shepherding perspective to bear upon all the operations and functions of church and minister, and draws conclusions of a theological order from reflection on these operations. (Hiltner 1958, 20)

An understanding of pastoral theology which begins with a study of the 'shepherding perspective', i.e. with the realities of pastoral practice, is obviously very different from the 'applied theology' approach discussed above. A preliminary and simplistic response might be that a study of practice cannot lead to any kind of theology but only to an anthropology or to a psychological understanding of human experience. However, a more detailed examination of Hiltner's argument reveals somewhat greater complexity. For Hiltner, all theological enquiry involves a relationship between faith and culture because when pastoral theology studies the insights of psychology, it is doing something intrinsic to theology. Faith can only remain faithful and relevant when it is in constant dialogue with culture. It is at this point that Hiltner engages with another of the theological giants of the twentieth century, namely Paul Tillich.

If Eduard Thurneysen's theology of pastoral care is congruent with the neo-orthodox theology of Karl Barth, Seward Hiltner's later theological method owes much to the thought of Paul

Tillich. Like Barth, Tillich's roots were in continental Europe, but he left Germany in 1933 and subsequently taught at Union Theological Seminary in New York as well as at Harvard and Chicago. As well as being a major systematic theologian, Tillich was one of the few of that discipline who engaged in a positive and constructive dialogue with modern psychology. Brooks Holifield (1983), author of the definitive history of pastoral care in America, makes the following assessment of his contribution to the discipline:

> Tillich also enhanced the understanding of pastoral care by his careful exploration of such notions as anxiety, freedom, guilt and courage. His work influenced the existential and phenomenological psychologists who sought to understand such themes without simply retracing them to childhood origins or viewing them as merely surface manifestations of deeper psychic processes. Tillich's single most important contribution to the theory of pastoral care might well have been his *The Courage to Be* (1952) in which he explored, among other topics, the relationship between ontological and pathological anxiety. (Holifield 1990, 1277)

Both Tillich and Hiltner were members of the New York Psychology Group, with obvious opportunities for the exchange of ideas. Crucial for our understanding of Hiltner, however, is Tillich's Principle of Correlation, published in his *Systematic Theology*, Volume 1, to which Hiltner acknowledges his indebtedness. Tillich writes:

> In using the method of correlation, systematic theology proceeds in the following way: it makes an analysis of the human situation out of which the existential questions arise, and it demonstrates that the symbols used in the Christian message are the answers to these questions. (Tillich 1951, 62)

The clear implication of this position is that culture, the pastoral event, the 'existential situation', poses the question, and the 'answer' to the problem is found within the symbols, the theological ideas which give expression to the Christian faith.

This, of course, is a position which is anathema to those who believe that the sole source of theological truth is to be found within the revelation, within the Christ-event, the Word of God incarnate, written and proclaimed. It can be argued, however, that Hiltner's work, proposing a dialectical relationship between theology and pastoral care, opened up a new chapter in pastoral theology. Certainly in a subsequent book, *Theological Dynamics* (1972), he demonstrated how certain concepts from both theology and psychology could be brought into a mutually critical relationship with one another. Whether or not he was the cause or even the catalyst in new approaches to pastoral theology is arguable. What is certain is that his work prefigured a time of excitement and ferment in practical theology as an academic discipline of which the theology of pastoral care is an integral part. Not only were new understandings of practical theology on the horizon, writers on both sides of the Atlantic were exploring new ways of relating theology more specifically to the practice of pastoral care.

So far in this chapter I have attempted to sketch the background to the contemporary debate in the theology of pastoral care. I began by looking at an understanding of the pastoral relationship with its roots in the neo-orthodox theology of Eduard Thurneysen. This was essentially a theology of the Word, and the pastoral care associated with it had a concern to bring the Word of God to bear upon the human situation. We then explored a very different understanding of the pastoral relationship which drew heavily upon the skills, the insights and the philosophies of a rapidly developing counselling movement with its origins mainly in post-war North America. There were undoubtedly teachers of pastoral care, those such as Carroll Wise and Seward Hiltner, who realized that there had to be some kind of relationship between theology and the exciting new therapeutic approaches. We have seen, particularly in the case of Hiltner, how over the years he continued to engage with the issue of the relationship between theology and pastoral care. The present state of play in this debate can only be understood in the light of a much larger discussion, and that is the rediscovery of practical theology itself as an academic and practical discipline.

REDISCOVERING PRACTICAL THEOLOGY

When John Foskett and I were engaged in writing our book on supervision and pastoral care we were looking for a way of describing the theological dimension of the supervisory process. I had been reading *The Promise of Narrative Theology* (1981) in which George Stroup argues that 'Revelation becomes an experienced reality at that juncture where the narrative identity of an individual collides with the narrative identity of the Christian community' (Foskett and Lyall 1988, 50). As we mulled over the possibility of developing this idea we felt that to talk of 'collision', of hard objects bouncing off one another leaving nothing but dents, did not quite catch the essence of the matter. It was at that point that the metaphor of the 'intercourse' of narratives began to commend itself. We felt that the sexual imagery portrayed more faithfully what was happening in the pastoral relationship as well as in supervision. In any such relationships there are various stories around, not only that of the person receiving pastoral care, but also that of the carer, and, of course, a pastoral relationship takes place in the context of a faith community which is shaped by its own story. Inevitably these stories interact with one another and become entwined. They penetrate one another in a process of mutual giving and receiving and out of this 'intercourse' there may be born something new, a new perspective on life or perhaps a new beginning free from the bondage of the past or, of course, a deepening of the relationship itself.

I want to argue that this way of relating theology and pastoral practice is significantly different from both of the models which I have already described as 'applied theology' and 'applied psychology'. More fundamentally, I want to locate this way of doing pastoral theology within an emerging, new understanding of practical theology, of the relationship between theology and practice. I have already indicated that within the past two decades there has been a revival of interest in practical theology. Concurrent with this development, and indeed closely related to it, we see also the emergence of other ways of bringing the Christian tradition to bear upon the realities of pastoral situations. The theology of pastoral care has also been influenced by two further developments which have come to play an important part on the wider theological scene. These are a revived interest in hermeneutics and the new insights which come from the nascent theologies of liberation. To these we will turn in due course, but first we must examine the broader phenomenon, namely the rebirth of practical theology as a theological discipline.

The need for a new approach to practical theology found expression in the formation of an International Academy of Practical Theology bringing together scholars from all over the world to meetings in Princeton (1993), Berne (1995), Seoul (1997) and Quebec City (1999). At a public meeting in Berne, James Fowler set out a definition of practical theology which embodies present understandings of the discipline. Practical theology, he writes, is

> Critical and constructive reflection by communities of faith
> Carried out consistently in the contexts of their praxis
> Drawing on their interpretations of normative sources from Scripture and tradition
> In response to their interpretations of the current challenges and situations they face, and
> Leading to on-going modifications and transformations of their practices
> In order to be more adequately responsive
> To their interpretation of the shape of God's call to partnership. (Fowler 1995, 4)

There are several features of this definition which help us to understand the nature of the new practical theology (and therefore of the theology of pastoral care). First, practical theology is an activity of the Church as community, exploration carried out in the context of a shared life and faith; second, it is an on-going activity of the Church in the light of its own praxis, i.e. its life and work arising out of its faith; third, practical theology cannot take place without engagement with an understanding of Scripture or theological tradition; fourth, interpretation and analysis of the current social/political reality is also integral to the nature of practical theology; fifth, practical theology does not exist for its own sake but ultimately to bring about a transformation in practice more congruent with an interpretation of the nature of discipleship.

The issues relate to both the content and the method. The subject matter of practical theology is not simply the professional tasks of the ordained ministry within the internal life of the Church. It also embraces reflection upon those critical issues in the world which affect the lives of all men and women and which set the context for the Church's witness. And the method is neither direct application of abstract theological principles nor what Bonhoeffer (quoting Nietzsche) called 'servile conviction in the face of the fact' (Bonhoeffer 1955, 198), an attitude which allows the Church's theology and practice to be shaped by an uncritical acceptance of the givenness of a situation. Rather, practical theology is a dynamic, critical branch of theology in a

dialectical relationship with contemporary culture, the theological tradition both being questioned by the realities of the
socio-political situation and in turn exercising a transformative
power within it.

The scope of the 'new' discipline of practical theology is
demonstrated in Paul Ballard and John Pritchard's *Practical
Theology in Action* (1996), subtitled *Christian Thinking in the
Service of Church and Society*. Practical theology is not simply the
Church talking to itself about itself. Practical theology is disci-
plined reflection upon the Church's interaction with society out
of the richness and diversity of its own tradition. From the wide
range of issues addressed by Ballard and Pritchard, three of a
general nature are worth exploring further. All relate to method
in practical theology. First, there is the *dialectical nature of
practical theology*. We saw, in the work of Thurneysen, both the
strengths and the weakness of the 'applied theology' model.
Positively, Christian action is located within the theological tradition; on the other hand, we saw that there can be 'no simple
deductive relationship between theology and practice' (Ballard
and Pritchard 1996, 60). In the work of Hiltner we noted the
beginning of correlational approaches to practical and pastoral
theology in which theology and practice engage with one
another – even 'play with' one another – so that out of that interaction new truths, or at least fresh insights, emerge. Ballard and
Pritchard list various ways in which this can be facilitated, some
of which are discussed below. Second, throughout *Practical
Theology in Action* there is liberal use of *case studies*. Practical
theology does not take place in a vacuum but is always engagement with and reflection upon the concrete situation. It is for
this reason that the present volume draws heavily upon the
lived experience of colleagues in ministry. Third, they stress the
centrality of theological reflection as integral to the nature of
practical theology, and we need to explore what this means.

THEOLOGICAL REFLECTION AND
THEOLOGICAL INTEGRATION

Ballard and Pritchard's discussion of this topic is closely related
to the ways in which theology may be related to practice (the
'models' for doing practical theology) but is not identical with
them. The 'models' approach relates to method in practical theology as an academic discipline and has its own importance.

'Theological reflection' is, however, more concerned with issues of personal integration. Conceptual frameworks may be devised to further the discipline of practical theology as an intellectual exercise, courses and curricula may be designed to provide an environment in which the process of theological integration takes place. At the end of the day, however, the locus of theological integration is the individual (or group). Our working theologies are highly personal constructs. We normally find ourselves within denominational families, we may identify ourselves with general theological positions, and are happy to confess our general allegiance to their traditions and statements of faith. Nevertheless, the actual working theologies which drive our actions are shaped not by credal statements (certainly not by credal statements alone) but by our experience of life. Within each of us there is a continuous internal dialogue taking place as we seek to relate present beliefs to fresh experience, allowing the emergence of a developing personal theology. One of the exercises in the Edinburgh MTh in Ministry is the writing of a major Theology of Ministry paper. From the outset, students have to be set free from imagining that the task is one of setting down on paper the theology of ministry which they think they ought to have – or that which they imagine the Church thinks they ought to have. Rather, the task is to liberate them to make explicit their implicit beliefs, to uncover the roots of their faith through exploring the influences, events, courses, books and people which have shaped their personal stories and spiritual journeys. In other words, they are invited to explore the extent to which their working theologies are shaped by their own stories. It is only then that they are asked to relocate their theology of ministry within their own ecclesiastical tradition. The outcome is normally a reaffirmation of the faith in which they stand, but owned at a much deeper level and open to the excitement of further development. Practical theology leads through theological reflection to theological integration.

We see, therefore, that theological reflection is only possible when we listen to the stories of individuals and communities as well as to the stories which have shaped the Church and its message. Two contemporary movements in theology embodying such insights have implications for a theology of pastoral care. The first is liberation theology, which will be discussed in the remainder of this chapter. The second explores the impact of the discipline of hermeneutics upon pastoral care.

LIBERATION THEOLOGY AND PASTORAL CARE

Liberation theology is a radically different way of doing theology. Emmanuel Lartey (1996) has identified three different approaches to practical theology, two of which we have already explored in some detail. His exposition of the *branch* approach is congruent with all that I have described above as 'applied theology' with its roots in Schleiermacher and bearing fruit in Thurneysen. His *process* approach encompasses the various 'correlational' methods originating in Tillich and developed by Hiltner and Tracy. Lartey expounds a third approach, what he calls the *'way of being and doing'* approach, of which liberation theology itself is a prime example.

Liberation theology, as commonly understood, has its origins in mid-twentieth-century Latin America in which the Church (predominantly Roman Catholic) allied itself with the struggles of ordinary people against poverty, oppression and Western domination. The Roman Catholic bishops meeting at Medellín, Colombia, in 1968 acknowledged that the Church had often sided with oppressive governments. From that point onwards the mission of the Church would be shaped by their conviction that 'God is clearly and unequivocally on the side of the poor' (Bonino 1997). Their starting point was that poverty and oppression were an affront both to the gospel of Jesus Christ and to the dignity of men and women. The liberation movements of Latin America saw it as their task to help people understand why things were as they were, to create within them the expectation that things could be better ('conscientization') and that ordinary people were capable of taking responsibility for change – indeed, that they had to do so. Theologically this led to new ways of reading the Bible, especially within the basic communities which were rapidly forming, drawing people from all walks of life. With its themes of exodus and liberation running through both Old and New Testaments, liberation theology found in the Bible paradigms totally relevant for the tasks of ministry which had to be undertaken amid the volatile and testing socio-political cauldron which was Latin America in the 1960s.

Liberation theology is a complex phenomenon and I merely draw attention to two features of it which are relevant for our exploration of themes in pastoral theology. First, as Lartey points out, liberation theology is essentially a way of doing theology, a method. It is certainly not 'applied theology' (as described in Chapter Two). Liberation theology does not start with either

Scripture or the propositional statements of the Western theological tradition. Rather, it starts with the actual socio-political
situation and enters into dialogue with Scripture and tradition:

> Liberation theology understands itself as critical reflection
> and action upon the vocation of ministry set forth in the
> gospel. It re-affirms the gospel's liberation of the poor and
> the oppressed, it argues that poverty must be examined as a
> systemic condition involving power relationships, and it
> asserts that poverty must be interpreted as the context of the
> total society in which the gospel is preached. Succinctly stated,
> authentic gospel-centered self-transformation necessitates the
> transformation of power relationships. (Moseley 1990, 645)

Second, the influence of liberation theology has not been confined to the transformation of the socio-political climate in Latin
America. Other situations of perceived oppression have drawn
upon the paradigms of liberation theology to provide a theological method with which to underpin their own struggles for
liberation. Feminist theology, whose growth has been most rapid
in North America but which is now of world-wide importance,
is a good example. In the final section of this chapter we shall
examine how two British scholars have constructed theologies
of pastoral care which are essentially liberation models. Stephen
Pattison has drawn extensively upon the insights of liberation
theology itself and Elaine Graham has addressed important
issues in pastoral theology from a feminist perspective.

A LIBERATION MODEL

Stephen Pattison is a distinguished pastoral theologian. His
Pastoral Care and Liberation Theology (1994/1997) is an excellent
exposition of the methods and insights of liberation theology
and of the light which they shed on some of the contemporary
issues in pastoral care. Liberation theology is a theology of
commitment. There can be no sitting on the fence in the face of
social injustice. Each of us must begin by asking the question
'Whose side am I on?' It is our answer to this question which
shapes our theological understanding. Pattison uses the methods
and insights to question whether or not pastoral care in Europe
and North America has concentrated too much on a psychotherapeutic model of care when it should have been directing its
energies to the social and political context of much human

distress. He argues that hospital chaplaincy has been shaped too much by secular counselling. An over-emphasis upon the pastoral care of individuals has led to a silencing of the prophetic warning which the Church should be uttering in the face of de-humanizing institutions.

While the starting point of liberation theology is a recognition of the Christian response which is required in the face of injustice, its methodology is essentially dialectical:

> The dialectical process may be seen as a circle whereby ideas, understandings and traditions, on the one hand, and actual practical action, on the other, continually enter into dialogue, stimulating and modifying each other. The concept of praxis contains the two-fold essence of action-reflection within it, Dialectical method within a praxis orientation is most clearly seen in Segundo's now-famous 'hermeneutical circle' . . . defined by Segundo as 'the continuing change in our interpretation of the Bible which is dictated by the continuing changes in our present day reality, both individual and social'. (Pattison 1997, 51)

Pattison is not unaware of the criticisms which have been made of liberation theology, that it is not in fact a theology at all, that it is more a method of social analysis or an ethic. He is also aware of the problem of 'experiential fundamentalism', the assumption that because something is true in the contextualized context of Latin America, it must be true for all Christians everywhere.

Alert to the problems of liberation theology, Pattison applies its insights to the pastoral care of patients in psychiatric hospitals within the British National Health Service. Starting with a social analysis of the condition of these patients, he begins to construct his own distinctive understanding of the pastoral role. Rather than be seduced by the individualistic model of care, chaplains should be challenging the structures which make the conditions of these patients so appalling, both those which lead to their admission and those which impede their recovery. There is much to applaud in this approach to the care of people; there are also important questions to be raised, particularly as regards his seeming rejection of more traditional patterns of pastoral care of the mentally ill. There is more than one way of exercising a prophetic ministry within an institution. Besides the public banner-waving kind of ministry which Pattison seems to advocate, there is a more subtle kind of ministry to structures based upon trusted human and pastoral relationships. The argument from silence is always a dangerous one. It is, however, quite conceivable that many problems and public scandals within institutions do not occur, precisely because a chaplain has been in the right place at the right time – an overwrought charge nurse helped through a personal difficulty before that difficulty is translated into patient abuse, or a senior manager helped to reflect upon a 'no win' decision so that the least damaging course of action is taken. I suspect that the chaplains who are trusted to function at this level are not those likely to be found on the picket lines or going public about the problems of the hospital. This is not to advocate silence in the face of blatant abuse. Chaplains have, however, many channels of protest open to them before going public. I suspect also that in many cases the kind of people who have the interpersonal skills which make good pastors are very different from the kind of people who make effective prophets – and vice versa!

FEMINIST PERSPECTIVES

Feminist theology is essentially a form of liberation theology. Its basic thesis is that both explicitly and implicitly the history of humankind has been dominated by patriarchal values. It has been a 'man's world' and until recently women have frequently colluded in this state of affairs. The feminist movement has over the past few years been engaged in the process of conscientization, of creating a new awareness of the oppression which has been, and still is, suffered by women simply because they are women. It is a movement which contains within it a rich diversity and it has had a profound influence upon the recent history of the Church. Some might consider that the debate about the ordination of women has been perhaps the most public manifestation of the impact of feminist perspectives upon Church and society. There have been, however, other equally important consequences. Fresh insights and energy have flowed from seeking to understand the Bible from a feminist perspective, from a thoroughgoing critique of the Western theological tradition incorporating the experience of women, and from new liturgies which have been both non-sexist and creative.

Pastoral care has inevitably been influenced by the feminist movement. Elaine Graham (1993) has pointed out two major deficiencies in traditional pastoral ministries. First of all, they were exercised, at least officially, only by men, who were the ordained 'shepherds of the flock'. The considerable pastoral gifts of women were either undervalued or totally ignored. But second, and of equal importance, the pastoral needs of women were either misunderstood or neglected:

> Vital areas of pastoral need for women – questions of abortion, contraception, child care, sexuality, violence and sexual abuse – only began to feature as legitimate pastoral concerns once women achieved greater visibility and entered positions of leadership in the churches. Women's unequal position in society has also gone unchallenged by the churches because pastoral theology has never been sufficiently client-centred to allow such critical perspectives to be articulated. (Graham 1993, 218)

Graham, citing James Grifis, identifies two possible models of pastoral theology. The traditional model of care they identify as 'Constantinian', which embodies principles like control, order and the authority of law. In contrast, the characteristics of a 'Liberation' model emphasize change, *metanoia* and innovation, and in this Graham sees a more appropriate vehicle for the embodiment of the insights and needs of women:

> Is it possible to see in the paradigm of pastoral practice as Liberation an effective model for the empowerment and pastoral care of women? A commitment to feminist praxis would mean modelling pastoral praxis on theological values and insights that promised the empowerment of women and addressed their pastoral needs; but also to see those pastoral relationships as reflections of the divine nature. Christian pastoral practice has the potential to reveal a God who is startlingly present in human encounter.

> ... liberationist and feminist perspectives ... emphasise the vulnerability of God through the suffering of Christ and identify the exclusion and pain of the poor and marginalised as experiences through which justice and redemption will be established. (Graham 1993, 222)

It has to be noted that Graham is not proposing a model of pastoral care which is to be exercised only by women or directed towards the needs of women. What is being proposed is a new way of doing pastoral care and a new way of thinking theologically about it which can illuminate the whole pastoral enterprise, practically and theologically. Drawing upon the insights of liberation theology, and that aspect of it which expresses the emerging feminist consciousness, we are offered a model of pastoral care which emphasizes risk, vulnerability, woundedness, context. It is a model which is inductive and correlational, in which the lived experience of women (and men) is brought into living encounter with the Christian tradition in ways which illuminate both.

In this chapter we have explored, in the context of a new paradigm for practical theology, different models for relating theology to pastoral practice. We cannot start with abstract theology and *apply* it to pastoral situations. And while the secular therapies undoubtedly have insights of value for pastoral practice, these insights do not in themselves help us to draw upon the rich tradition of the Church's pastoral practice. We have noted recent developments in practical theology, in particular the emergence of liberation theology, both for their own importance and for the fresh light which they shed upon the relationship between theology and pastoral care. We shall devote the next chapter to exploring the implications of another significant development in theology for pastoral theology, namely the science of hermeneutics and its implications for understanding both the Christian story and the stories of people's lives.

CHAPTER THREE

Understanding Stories

In the last chapter I described how students are encouraged to integrate an understanding of the story of their lives into their own personal understanding of ministry. This does not mean, however, that one can simply explore one's own experience and feelings and call that theology. Independent of one's own story there are other stories embedded in Scripture and in the history and shared life of the community of faith. How are we to understand all these stories? And how do they help to shape our understanding of pastoral practice? We turn, therefore, to an examination of the relationship between narrative and pastoral care. We shall do this both theoretically and by analysis of one pastoral relationship captured in a case study.

When two very disparate disciplines find that a certain theme is generating interest within them separately, it is inevitable that those who work at the interface of these disciplines should wish to explore the bridge-building potential of that theme. In recent years within both theology and psychotherapy there has been considerable interest in the role of narrative or story, and as a consequence this has become an important theme in pastoral theology, working as it does on the boundary of theology and the human sciences.

In theology itself, narrative has come to be seen by many as an important vehicle for the communication of truth. John Bowden (1983, 391) sees this development as a consequence of problems perceived in more traditional and propositional modes of theological communication, such as creeds, confessions and dogmatic statements, together with an appreciation of the insights into human nature to be found in classical literature up to and including the modern novel. This, however, has a deeper implication than the idea that in stories there is the possibility of illustrating

44

theological truths regarded essentially as propositional. Rather, there is the 'stronger suggestion that narrative or *story* is a means of expression uniquely suited to theology or at least to Christian theology' (McLendon 1974, 188). It can be argued that much of 'the Christian fact' has a narrative quality. The Old Testament tells the story of Israel prior to the birth of Jesus Christ (and to see the Hebrew Bible in this light implies a certain hermeneutic). The Old Testament itself is full of good stories – not simply stories 'with morals' but stories which in their telling and hearing disclose something of the human condition. In the New Testament we have four different stories of the life of Jesus Christ, which are in effect four different interpretations of his life. It is a statement of the obvious to say that Jesus taught by making use of stories, but again, more recent understanding of the parables has moved beyond seeing the parables as illustrations of general truths about God and humankind to seeing them as possessing their own power to disclose both the realities of human life and the radical nature of God's grace. Sallie TeSelle writes:

> Why does everyone love a good story and how is story related to theological reflection? The answer to these two questions is I believe related. We all love a good story because of the narrative quality of human experience; in a sense any story is about ourselves, and a *good* story is good precisely because it rings true to human life . . . We recognise our own pilgrimages from here to there in a good story; we feel its movement in our bones and know it is 'right' . . . We love stories, then, because our lives are stories and we recognise in the attempts of others to move, temporally and painfully, our own story . . . For the Christian, the story of Jesus is *the* story par excellence. That God should be with us in a story of a human life could be seen as a happy accident, but it makes more sense to see it as God's way of always being with human beings *as they are*, as the concrete temporal beings who have a beginning and an end – who are, in other words, stories themselves. (TeSelle 1975, 159)

In tune with these ideas I will, in Chapter Five, attempt to construct a theology of pastoral care in which biblical narrative (including 'the story of Jesus') is central. It should be noted, however, that Sallie TeSelle (or McFague) published this paper in 1975 prior to the onset (or perhaps just the popularizing) of the debate about postmodernism. One of the main planks of post-modernism is to assert that the 'big stories' identified by Crites (1971) and affirmed by McFague no longer hold sway in contemporary culture. Before proceeding to constructive work on a theology of pastoral care, therefore, it will be necessary (in Chapter Four) to examine the postmodern critique of 'big stories' or *metanarratives* such as the Christian gospel.

In psychology, too, narrative approaches have begun to find a place. Gordon Lynch (1997) points out that while this is not a dominant trend, three significant developments can be identified. First, Kenneth Gregen (Lynch 1997) makes a distinction between micro-narratives which describe specific events in our lives (e.g. what happened yesterday) and macro-narratives (e.g. family background) which make sense of our lives on a broader level. There is a close relationship between how people describe their immediate past experience and their broader worldview. Second, David Epston and Michael White (Lynch 1997) describe the process of narrative psychology as one in which clients replace existing stories of themselves that are problematic with stories that allow them to live more satisfactorily. This process of recon-structing stories about themselves helps clients see themselves and their lives in a different light. Third, psychoanalyst Donald Spence (Lynch 1997) has argued that the role of the therapist is to enable the patient to find a 'narrative home' for his or her experience.

> According to Spence, the purpose of the therapeutic process is to help clients find meaningful stories within which they are able to make sense of experiences which may be anomalous, painful or puzzling. The ultimate test of a narrative created through the therapeutic process is not its historical truthful-ness . . . Rather the efficacy of the narrative developed through the analysis rests on its aesthetic quality, that is its ability to make sense of a client's experience meaningfully or satisfy-ingly. (Lynch 1997, 11)

The following story of ministry comes from Ruth, a woman who is both a minister and the wife of a minister:

> Jim is 16, a member of the congregation in which I, the minister's wife, worship. His older sisters, parents and grandparents also worship in that same church, and over the years our two families have built up a close friendship.

Jim helps to run our Youth Fellowship. Recently Jim rang and asked if he might talk to me. It transpired that he had been the victim of homosexual rape at a friend's house, for which awful experience he was receiving professional therapy and legal representation. But as I listened it became clear that beneath the feelings of uncleanness, his loss of self-worth and his desire to run away from all existing relationships, was something else – a deep anger with his parents for 'letting' this happen. Knowing his background as I already did – knowing the care and the love with which he and his sisters have been surrounded all their lives, and his parents' struggle to let Jim, the least academically able, have the same opportunities in life as the others – I was able to take a much more rounded view of the situation than I might have done if I had only known Jim.

Together we gently explored the huge theme of freedom-in-love. I found myself bringing to those discussions a whole raft of material, such as:

- my own 'stories' of being a daughter brought up quite restrictively, and of being the mother of a near-adolescent daughter – my constant battle with myself as I watch her breaking away from the nest and long to hold her back (Jim was able to smile at this knowing my family as he does!);
- that last wonderful line from C. Day Lewis' poem 'Walking Away';
- my undergirding trust in a heavenly Parent who gives us freedom to 'go to a different country' (Luke 15.13) in order that we may grow up; indeed, my belief in a God who allows the possibility of failure and of new beginnings.

There was what I can only call a visible moment of disclosure when first I touched upon the awful balancing act that all parents – and our Parent – must negotiate between loving protectively and letting go in love. For him it was a moment when his outlook on his parents' involvement in the experience changed; for me, it brought a new understanding of God's suffering as a Parent. A new frame for both our lives was opened up as the three stories merged; it was a moment of advent, of parabolic subversion. And for Jim, real healing began then.

We have had further conversations since then, but not at pre-arranged times; rather, we have talked in the course of on-going parish life – over a burger at the summer bar-becue, after a film which the Youth Fellowship watched together, and so on – thus allowing Jim to take the initiative and continue the process as and when he wished. Such a seemingly 'casual' way of handling things seemed to please him, contrasting as it did with the more rigorous approach of the legal consultants and professional therapists he was also seeing at that time. It was one, moreover, in which Jim did not have to do much preliminary 'explaining' about himself or his family in order to be understood.

In this case we note, first of all, that Ruth tells a good story. Her description of the relationship with Jim is no mere recounting of the facts. We learn more than the fact of the homosexual rape; we are also given a sense of what this event has done to him as a person. And we get a sense of his wider context, of his ambiva-lence about his family, of the contradiction between their (apparent) care for him and his (apparently) irrational blaming of them for what had happened to him. We learn of the 'more rounded' view which Ruth, as a pastor, has of this situation than might be available to a counsellor. And if Ruth is able to open up Jim's story to us, she is no less forthcoming about her own story. We are given an insight into the ambivalent feelings which she has experienced as both a daughter and a mother, of the tensions experienced during her own restricted upbringing now replayed a generation on but in the opposite role. We are also aware that this story is set in the context of a wider story. For that context is a community of faith, formed by a story which is both the story of the congregation in that place and at that time and the grand narrative of the Christian Church stretching back over two millennia. This context is important. In contrast to a counselling relationship, the pastoral relationship is on-going, informal and unstructured. Boundaries are somewhat confused but that is the nature of pastoral relationships. Ruth may be perceived by Jim as *a* minister but not *the* minister, wife of the minister and friend of his parents. Strangely, it is within the essential messiness of this situation that all these stories begin to engage with one another and effective pastoral care actually takes place.

The critical moment in this relationship is described by Ruth as a 'visible moment of disclosure when first I touched upon the awful balancing act that all parents – and our Parent – must negotiate between loving protectively and letting go in love'. This was certainly not non-directive counselling. Advocates of the 'rule of abstinence', counsellors who never share anything of themselves, would be horrified. It was, however, a sharing of vulnerability and it led to a moment of disclosure for both Jim and Ruth. For Jim there was new, perhaps his first, understanding of what it meant to be a parent. For Ruth it was a deeper understanding of God's suffering as a parent. For neither was there any change in the facts of the situation. For both there was a new way of interpreting these facts, of making sense of their own story.

There are more insights to be found in this story, especially in relation to Ruth's ministry as a woman. It is perhaps worth pointing out that Ruth, the narrator of this story, is no theological neophyte. It is not every minister's wife (nor indeed every minister) who is familiar with the concept of parabolic subversion. Ruth brings a high level of theological sophistication to her understanding of what is going on in this pastoral relationship, which is congruent with Elaine Graham's feminist perspective. First of all, Ruth brought to the pastoral relationship something of her own story, her experience of being a daughter 'brought up quite restrictively'; and she brought her experience of being the mother of a near-adolescent girl about to spread her wings. Second, she took the risk of sharing this with Jim, of making herself vulnerable. A client-centred counsellor or psychotherapist would almost certainly not have shared as much of herself. It could have gone badly wrong but in the event her intuition was right and the sharing of her own dilemma, especially as a parent, opened up for Jim a new way of interpreting his parents' attitude to him. In Ruth's basic trust in a heavenly Parent who gives us freedom to go into a far country, Jim found space in which to grow up, to fail and make new beginnings. In Jim's telling of his story and in Ruth's perceptive hearing of it, Jim was able to reinterpret the story and find a new meaning for his life, a new 'narrative home' for his experience. We now turn to a slightly more technical discussion of the relationship between pastoral care and the interpretation of stories.

PASTORAL CARE AS HERMENEUTICS

Hermeneutics as applied to the interpretation of ancient texts and documents has a long and well-established history. There has, however, been a great broadening in the scope of hermeneutics, with attempts to devise methods of interpreting contemporary situations as well as ancient texts. It was Wilhelm Dilthey (1833–1911) who first found in the discipline of hermeneutics the foundation of all disciplines that interpret expressions of the inner life of humans, whether those be human actions, law, art or literature. More recently, Paul Ricoeur (1981) has extended the principles of hermeneutics into the social sciences. This development has been of particular importance for recent developments in pastoral care. The 'father' of the modern pastoral care movement is generally reckoned to be Anton Boisen who in 1926, while chaplain at Worcester State Hospital in Massachusetts, invited a group of theological students to work with him in the hospital over the summer. He did so with the conviction that there was no better laboratory for the study of people in crisis than the mental hospital and no better library than the 'living human documents', a phrase that has come of be of critical importance in pastoral education and theology. It is not a long step from the consideration of people as 'living human document' to an approach to the understanding of people which might be described as 'hermeneutic'. It is arguable that the purpose of pastoral care and counselling is, at least in part, to help people gain a greater understanding of the stories of their lives, to interpret their stories in a new way, and on the basis of that fresh understanding to find their lives transformed. Two North American authors, Donald Capps of Princeton Theological Seminary and Charles Gerkin from the Candler School of Theology in Atlanta, have been particularly creative in taking methods first applied to the interpretation of written texts and applying them to the finding of meaning in the stories which embody human experience and pastoral activity.

DONALD CAPPS, PAUL RICOEUR AND MEANINGFUL PASTORAL ACTION

We noted earlier that the French philosopher Paul Ricoeur applied hermeneutic principles to the human sciences. In turn, Capps in his *Pastoral Care and Hermeneutics* (1984) borrowed basic concepts from Ricoeur and used them as a framework on which to construct a theological interpretation of pastoral ministry. Ricoeur had pointed out significant parallels between meaningful (as opposed to random) human action and written texts. This, argues Capps, has consequences for our understanding of pastoral care, assuming that it is a category of meaningful human action. Ricoeur had argued as follows:

First, like written texts, meaningful action leaves its mark. The written word not only has content, it has an impact upon those who read it. From a reading of both the ancient Scriptures and the modern novel, people have been moved, often emotionally, sometimes spiritually and on occasion to take action. Likewise, a pastoral act has both content and consequences. Words are spoken and heard and they leave their impact, for better or for worse, on everyone involved: on the pastor, on the cared for and upon those who hear the words or hear about them. A colleague in ministry tells the following story:

> An elder phoned in tears to ask me to call in an emergency. Her daughter had just told her she was pregnant out of wedlock. I was able soon to say to her, 'Is it not wonderful that God has blessed your daughter with a baby; new life is come into the world, bringing joy.' That was many years ago. The grandmother (as she now is) came back to me quite recently to remind me and tell me what a healing word it was for her.

Second, like written texts, meaningful action has unintended consequences. Texts sometimes are experienced as having meaning never intended by the author. This is certainly true of the Scriptures, different people finding parts of the Bible uniquely meaningful for them. And it is certainly true of sermons. Preachers universally have experienced a reaction to something which they were not aware of having said. The following, not atypical, story is told by a minister preaching in a neighbouring congregation.

> I was preaching on the Fatherhood of God. In the midst of the sermon a young woman apparently took ill and was led from the church. Later, her friends simply said that she had 'problems'. I reported the incident to my colleague as parish minister. He looked knowingly and said nothing except that he would follow it up.
> Three years later, a young woman appeared in my church. She identified herself as the person who took ill in the previous incident. She wanted to speak with me privately. Conversations revealed that she had been sexually

abused by her father. The preaching on the Fatherhood of God had been too much to bear. Nonetheless, the incident had been an important point of admitting the truth to herself. Further counselling saw her through to a place of healing.

Third, like written texts, meaningful action creates a world. Ricoeur maintains that while spoken communication takes place within a world which is already shared, written discourse opens up new worlds for us. Thus 'texts speak of possible worlds and of possible ways of orienting oneself in these worlds' (Capps 1984, 38). Similarly, intentional action creates new worlds. A couple's declaration of their intention to marry not only has immediate consequences. It also creates new worlds for them, their families and their friends, which only become apparent with the passage of the years. Similarly with pastoral actions. Capps describes a situation in which a pastor attempts to assure two sisters, not present at the death of their father, that the old man had died fully lucid. The consequence (unintended) was to provoke bad feeling between the two women, who had disagreed about whether or not they should remain with their father on that last night. It also created new opportunities for pastoral ministry.

Fourth, like written texts, meaningful action is always open to reinterpretation. The written word has the possibility of being reinterpreted by anyone who can read. Similarly, new meanings in any given action may be discovered which were not seen by the original agent or by people who were not there. According to Ricoeur, fresh interpretations are most compelling when they lead not only to new thinking but to fresh praxis. Thus Capps describes how the pastor mentioned above visited one of the daughters not present at the father's death and, on gently exploring with her the immediate disagreement with her sister, uncovered a story of deep and long-standing conflict between the two women.

It is the possibility of the reinterpretation of meaningful action which makes possible both preparation for ministry and professional growth in ministry. Ricoeur makes the further point that there are no privileged interpreters in relation to a text. In fact, later readers may see things not obvious to either the author or the original readers. In its application to meaningful action, the whole process of Clinical Pastoral Education depends upon this insight. Typically, a student will write up a verbatim account of a pastoral situation which is then discussed in a peer-group setting in which various things may happen. As she presents her report, the student may well see aspects of the situation which she did not see even in the 'writing up' stage. Her peers may also begin to identify further issues which illuminate both the situation under discussion and other pastoral situations in which they have been involved. Further, a powerful form of continuing education for ministry is the case study approach (Northcott 1990) in which pastors are prepared to share their experiences of ministry in an open and undefended manner.

Central to the work of both Capps and Ricoeur is the issue of pastoral integrity. The latter has pointed out that three of the great thinkers who influenced the twentieth century, Marx, Nietzsche and Freud, have each in their own way argued that Christianity has its origins in an illusory view of reality. All pastoral actions, therefore, are examples of a 'false consciousness' because the Christian community is built around these false perceptions of reality. And so at one level there can be no integrity in pastoral care without a satisfactory response to these critiques. It can be argued that the postmodern critique of metanarratives, of 'grand stories' such as the Christian story, is a contemporary manifestation of this critique, and this will be examined in detail in the next chapter. Capps, however, addresses the issue of pastoral integrity in terms of a more modest series of questions.

1 Is there an essential congruence between the pastor's intentionality in the action itself and the action's appropriation by others?
2 Is the pastor's praxis, as reflected in this action, a true reflection of his or her pastoral self-understanding?
3 Do the world-disclosive possibilities of the action address the fundamental human desires of the individuals for whom they are intended? (Capps 1984, 58)

Capps is therefore locating pastoral integrity in the congruence between the minister's intentions, her actions, their reception by those for whom they are intended and the appropriateness of the pastoral action in terms of meeting their real needs. In the first vignette of ministry cited above (in which the elder was distressed because of her daughter's pregnancy) there was indeed an essential congruence between the minister's intention and its appropriation by the woman. *This* minister knew exactly what needed to be said to *this* woman. (We cannot assume that this comment would have been universally helpful.) Further, what the minister did, his praxis, was indeed a reflection of his pastoral self-understanding, one whose calling was to mediate the love of God. Finally, his pastoral action disclosed a different world from what the woman expected and feared. A world feeding upon shame and petty gossip was replaced by one nurtured by acceptance and grace and joy. The world disclosed by the minister's comments was one which met her deepest needs. Contrast this with another story told by the same minister.

> I visited a hospital every day for a week, morning and night, to pray at the bedside of a man in a coma who had attempted suicide. On day six he wet the bed and the nurses rejoiced; on day eight he opened his eyes, and when I saw him on day nine he was groggy but alive and going to survive. He cursed me for being a busybody, for he had absconded with goods and would be going to prison. You can't win them all!

Manifestly there was no congruence between the minister's action and its appropriation by the man who had tried to take his own life. The minister prayed for life; the man wanted to die. Certainly the minister's intervention was a true reflection of his pastoral self-understanding. After all, ministers are expected to pray for healing. (I pass no judgement on the efficacy of intercessory prayer and the relative contributions of medical and spiritual interventions to the process of recovery.) Finally, the world disclosed by the minister's intervention (assuming that prayer contributed at least in part to his recovery) did not address the desire of the one for whom it was intended. The man desired death and whatever he imagined that held for him; the world disclosed was that of imprisonment and shame and disgrace. Does this mean that in the second case the minister acted with less pastoral integrity than in the first? After all, it was the same minister acting in both situations. Here we might question Capps' use of the words 'fundamental human desires'. It verges on the unacceptably judgemental to say that pastoral interventions must be directed towards fundamental human needs rather than desires. There is an arrogance in ministers claiming to know what is best for people. Yet there are few ministers who have not experienced the subtle manipulation of people who know what they want, whether or not the minister is able or willing to deliver. Normally, when both parties have a degree of self-awareness, the sometimes complex relationship between needs and desires is one which can be explored in the course of the pastoral conversation. Perhaps it was not unreasonable of the minister to assume that behind the attempted suicide there was the near-universal instinct for survival and that he would have been lacking in pastoral integrity if he had not prayed for healing. Finally, we cannot but be impressed by the minister's diligence in this situation – but such is the stuff of good parish ministry.

CHARLES GERKIN, HANS-GEORG GADAMER AND THE FUSION OF HORIZONS

While Donald Capps builds his hermeneutic theology of pastoral care through engagement with ideas from the French philosopher Paul Ricoeur, Charles Gerkin's main dialogue partner is the German philosopher Hans-Georg Gadamer. Gerkin is a professor of pastoral psychology steeped in the American tradition of pastoral counselling which we noted above. The title of the work in which he explores the relationship between hermeneutics and pastoral care, *The Living Human Document: Re-Visioning Pastoral Counseling in a Hermeneutic Mode* (1984), is borrowed directly from Anton Boisen, generally regarded as the father of the modern pastoral counselling movement. Gerkin's basic presuppositions are two-fold. First,

> Pastoral counselors are, more than anything else, listeners to and interpreters of stories. Persons seek out a pastoral counselor because they need someone to listen to their story. (Gerkin 1984, 26)

Second, however, the pastoral counsellor is more than someone who listens to stories.

> He or she is also a bearer of stories and of a story. The pastoral counselor does not come empty-handed to the task of understanding the other's story and offering the possibility of a new interpretation. The pastoral counselor brings his or her own interpretation of life experience. (Gerkin 1984, 27)

This is not an easy process because communication has to take place across at least two language barriers, not only that which exists *between* the counsellor and the counsellee but also that *within* the counsellor himself as he tries to understand what is going on within the counsellee (and perhaps himself) psychologically, theologically and in terms of any other conceptual framework which might be relevant. Gerkin begins by recounting something of his own journey in ministry. This is no narcissistic introduction to his writing but is integral to his argument. A son of the manse, he himself first encountered the new emerging psychological approaches to pastoral care during a course in seminary and went on to train as a pastoral counsellor at the highest level. In due course he became aware that methods of training in pastoral counselling with their focus upon the personhood of the counsellor were turning the pastoral care movement in a therapeutic direction. What consideration was being given to theological understandings of pastoral care was minimal:

> theological reflection can in that situation become like the bumper sticker slapped on the bus as it is pulling out of the parking lot on its way to a psychologically determined destination. (Gerkin 1984, 17)

His concern, therefore, is for a recovery of pastoral counselling's theological roots. This is, however, a concern for more than a recovery of theological language; he wishes to promote deep and genuine engagement between the language systems of psychology and theology in relation to the realities of pastoral practice. He finds his tool for this task in hermeneutics because

> a hermeneutical perspective sees all human language systems, including both theology and psychology, as efforts to penetrate the mystery of what is beyond human understanding and to make sense of it. (Gerkin 1984, 19)

Among the many hermeneutical traditions, it was within the thought of the contemporary German philosopher Hans-Georg Gadamer that Gerkin found a congenial model for pastoral theological reflection. For Gadamer, the hermeneutic task is essentially a dialogical process in which what is hoped for is a 'fusion of horizons of understanding and meaning' (Gerkin 1984, 44). There can be no 'objective' examination of either a text or a human situation as if one could stand apart from the historical process and pass judgement from a position of neutrality. Rather, we bring to every situation, our prejudices, our 'pre-understandings'. Each of us has in any given situation a 'horizon of understanding'.

> The important thing is to be aware of our own bias, so that the text may present itself in all its newness and thus be able to assert its own truth against one's own fore-meanings. (Gerkin 1984, 45)

The application of the concept of 'a horizon of understanding' to pastoral care has several consequences:

First, it points to the finite limits within which we work in an effort to understand the other person. Even empathy, that most basic of Rogerian concepts deemed essential to a good helping relationship, has its limits. Empathy is not simply a technique which can be applied by the counsellor or carer. Our own capacity for understanding is bounded by the horizon of our own experience. In caring for another we open up the horizons of our understanding to admit the intrusion of the world of the other. We allow our understandings to be challenged in the hope that something new may be shared in the encounter so that our capacity for understanding may be extended.

Second, it allows pastoral counselling to move beyond the mind-set taken over from the scientific-technological world of most of the secular helping professions. Pastoral care and counselling are far more than the application of learned techniques to the solving of human problems. Rather, such techniques as are used must serve as a vehicle for sharing the beliefs and values which they hold in common. Techniques can both impede and facilitate understanding of the 'text' of the living human document.

Third, it contains the possibility that both the interpreter and the object of interpretation may be changed at the fundamental level of meaning. The fusion of horizons opens up a new and novel vision of possibility, a new and novel opening into what might be, as indicated in the following story recounted by a woman priest.

> This happened while I was a deacon. For some obscure reason, a deacon in the Anglican Church is not permitted to give a blessing. A close friend and neighbour, a practising and devout Roman Catholic who had from time to time

attended services in our church, was dying of cancer and was aware that she had only a few weeks to live. When I visited her, she asked me for a blessing. Being a law-abiding person and an inexperienced deacon, I steadfastly refused and said that much as I would like to this was not a possibility. Fortunately, as her death approached, I realized how much it would mean to her and how absurd my scruples were in God's eyes. The resultant occasion was one of great poignancy and significance for both of us.

This situation from the early ministry of an Anglican priest shows how the idea of the 'fusion of horizons' may help us to understand what is going on in the pastoral relationship. For this priest-in-training, her horizon was limited by her loyalty to her Church's teaching about the giving of blessings. Yet the world of her dying friend continued to intrude and to undermine her pre-understandings of this aspect of ministry. Eventually some kind of 'fusion of horizons' took place. Both women were changed by this pastoral action which 'was one of poignancy and significance for both of us'. The dying woman had received a blessing and we can only guess how significant it was for her that she had received it from the hands of her friend and neighbour. The deacon's understanding of the nature of blessing was broadened. Perhaps also she came to a new understanding of herself as a person and a minister, because in a covering letter she says how intrigued she was to note that in this situation 'technically she had broken the rules'. How liberating she found it to realize that she could break rules!

For Gerkin, while good pastoral practice depends upon the fusion of the horizons of carer and cared for, a theological understanding of this practice depends upon a fusion of the horizons of psychological theory and theological insight. In this chapter we have explored models which facilitate this process. In a most recent book, Gerkin, drawing upon the work of the Yale theologian George Lindbeck, provides I believe an admirable way of summing up my argument so far and of taking the discussion to a more profound, but essentially simpler, level.

GEORGE LINDBECK, THE NATURE OF DOCTRINE AND PASTORAL CARE

In his *Introduction to Pastoral Care* (1997), written in his retirement, Gerkin reviews the story of his own journey in pastoral care and counselling, and he does so in the context of the recent history of a movement in which he has been one of the significant figures. Having been at the forefront of the pastoral counselling movement for the past generation, it is clear that Gerkin is moving beyond the psychotherapeutic paradigm of ministry and is (re)locating pastoral care in a theological context in which the Christian narrative is foundational. It is within the theological framework of George Lindbeck that Gerkin finds a framework in which to express his self-understanding as a pastor.

In *The Nature of Doctrine*, Lindbeck distinguishes three under-standings of doctrine, two of which we have already encountered as manifestations of particular approaches to the theology of pastoral care. These are the *propositionalist*, the *experiential-expressivist* and the *cultural-linguistic*. In the propositionalist understanding of doctrine, truth is expressed in precise verbal formulations, in creeds and confessions. On this view, theological statements are not poetic or metaphoric; they bear a direct cor-respondence with that to which they refer, and faith is a matter of giving total allegiance to the verbal formulations themselves. It will be obvious that this is the kind of theology which lies behind the theology of pastoral care set out by Eduard Thurneysen whose approach was discussed above.

The experiential–expressivist approach to doctrine is, on the other hand, decidedly an expression of modernity. Its roots are in the 'liberal' theologies of the nineteenth and twentieth centuries. Theologically, human experience not only raises the existential questions but hopefully (perchance) finds something in the theological tradition which confirms the experience. It was this way of doing theology which lay behind much of the burgeoning pastoral counselling movement of mid-twentieth-century North America and international developments which had their roots in that movement. Gerkin writes:

> Twentieth-century pastoral care's focus on the concrete experience of individuals and families has quite naturally, if often self-consciously, lent itself to a sometimes rough-hewn experiential–expressivist dialogue between the specifics of an encountered human experience and the meanings of certain theological symbols. Most often the common human experi-ence has been described in psychological language and then a theological symbol that correlates with this psychologically denoted symbol has been sought. (Gerkin 1997, 107)

The critique of these two approaches offered by Gerkin provides another way of restating the criticisms already made of Thurneysen on the one hand and of earlier North American approaches on the other. If the one leads to a pastoral theology which is essentially dominated by a propositional theology unrelated to human experience, the other leads to an understanding of pastoral care dominated by psychological categories and largely devoid of theological content. It is in the cultural–linguistic theology of George Lindbeck that Gerkin finds the basis for a more adequate theology of pastoral care (and, as we shall see, James Fowler finds a more adequate response to the experience of postmodernism).

What then does Lindbeck mean by a cultural–linguistic model? Gerkin describes it in the following terms:

> Whereas propositionalist modes of doing theology may be seen as analogous to science (theology as science seeks to assert facts about reality), and experiential-expressivism as analogous to poetry and the arts (theology as art or poetry seeks to express what human beings universally experience), the cultural–linguistic model of doing theology is analogous to culture (theology as the attempt to objectify a particular religious culture and its embodiment in narrative and ritual). (Gerkin 1997, 108)

The Bible is seen not as a set of propositional statements but as 'the grounding narrative of a religious community that seeks to structure its life according to the sacred truths contained in that narrative' (Gerkin 1997, 109). Lindbeck's problems with the experiential-expressivist position are two-fold. First, he doubts that there is a common, universal core of human experience which shapes the religious quest. As we shall see, the whole point of postmodernism is that the pluralism of cultural experience in fact creates very diverse experiences for individuals. Second, the experiential-expressivist theologies assume a very individualistic religious experience from which individuals move out in search of community. In fact, argues Lindbeck, the reverse is true. Religious experience is primarily communal rather than individualistic. Belonging to a community constituted by a story takes precedence over believing the story itself. This has profound implications for our understanding of the nature of pastoral care.

The cultural–linguistic model of doing theology is the most fundamental model by which a community can care for individuals and families. It has the unique ability to provide people with a storied context of ultimate meaning for their lives. To the degree that this storied context maintains its connection with all the varied stories of individual, family and community life in the world, it can provide a meaning-filled nesting place and thus provide the most elementary context of care . . . Practical theology becomes the task of maintaining the connections between the varied stories of life and the grounding story of the Christian community. (Gerkin 1997, 110)

Gerkin describes this model of care as a 'narrative–hermeneutic' model, its structure emphasizing both the human penchant for structuring life according to stories and the power of interpretation to shape life and express care. He schematizes this model as follows:

The story of the Christian community and its tradition	Pastoral care	The particularity of life stories

Thus 'pastoral care is the dialogical space between the communal story of the Christian community and the many life stories of many people who are in some way related to the Christian community' (Gerkin 1997, 112).

Those who would be pastors within the community of faith will always live in the tension between loyalty to the narrative which constitutes that community and an empathic response to the particularity of the very human stories of those who are hurting. Rejecting a propositionalist approach to pastoral care, believing that there must be a 'word' for every situation, pastors will nevertheless be aware of the rich resources for fresh perspectives contained in Christian narrative and worship. Sceptical of the idea that within the human psyche alone there is the source for healing, pastors know that there can be no healing without deep listening to particular human stories of hurt and despair and hope and self-acceptance – and that sometimes in the telling of the story there is a balm.

Pastors must exercise ministry in the tension between the story of the Christian community and its tradition and the particularity of individual life stories. The lives of individuals and communities are lived out amid the complexities of contemporary society. That society is often described as 'postmodern'. In the next chapter we shall explore the meaning of this term and what it means for pastoral ministry. Two main questions will concern us. What is the nature of this so-called postmodern society which is the context for ministry? And what are the implications of postmodernism for our understanding of the Christian story which is foundational for the theology and practice of pastoral care advocated in the chapters which follow?

CHAPTER FOUR

The Challenge of Postmodernism

In the previous two chapters I described some contemporary models for relating theology to practice. I wish, in due course, to set out a theology of pastoral care which, on the one hand, is rooted in the Christian narrative and, on the other hand, takes seriously the social and cultural situation within which ministry must be exercised. The understanding of pastoral care which I have already set out presupposes that it is care given and received within the matrix of relationships which constitute a community of faith, in this case the Christian Church. At the centre of this community of faith are the events surrounding the life and death of Jesus of Nazareth. We must explore how these events, which happened so long ago, impinge upon contemporary pastoral practice. These events, however, important as they are in their own right, do not stand alone. They have antecedents located within the history of the Jewish people and witnessed to in the Hebrew Bible. Further, much followed from these events, nothing less than Christendom itself, at the heart of which is the history of the Church. That history is replete with stories of witness and apostasy, and the perennial struggle of the Church to restate its faith through creed and confession in ways which engaged seriously with the culture and philosophy of each succeeding generation. In short, the events and experience which constitute the Christian Church have an intensely narrative quality. The story of the Jewish people, the story of the man Jesus and the stories which he told, and the story of the community formed in response to the story of Jesus, all point to a 'grand narrative' which has had a profound influence not only upon individuals but upon the whole of human history. There can be no theology of pastoral care which does not engage with this narrative.

I have argued, however, that the theology of pastoral care is part of the wider discipline called practical theology which is essentially dialectical in character. In Chapter Two, for example, we saw how Hiltner based his theology of pastoral care upon Tillich's analysis of the relationship between theology and culture. Therefore, as well as grounding our understanding of pastoral care in the narrative which constitutes the community of faith we must also seek to understand the wider culture within which that community 'lives and moves and has its being'.

A word which is often used to characterize contemporary society is 'postmodern'. There are two reasons why we must seek some understanding of this term. The first is a general one. If it is considered an appropriate description of the age in which we live, then there can be no dialectical theology of pastoral care which does not seek to engage with what that word or idea is trying to express about the present time. The second reason is that there is one particular feature of postmodernism which is of special significance for *this* enterprise, for the construction of a theology of pastoral care grounded in the narrative identity of a community of faith. A central tenet of postmodernism relates to what has been called 'the eclipse of metanarrative', the hypothesis that there is, in fact, no single 'grand story' on which we can base our understanding of the nature of things. And so, by way of clearing the ground, we will need to examine how far the postmodern critique of metanarratives inhibits us from constructing a theology of pastoral care rooted in the story of Jesus Christ.

POSTMODERN SOCIETY AS THE CONTEXT OF CONTEMPORARY MINISTRY

What exactly is postmodernism? The postmodern thesis is that we are now experiencing a major shift in our perception of how things are. Until recently we perceived ourselves as living in 'modern times'. These times have, in fact, been with us for a long time. They have their roots in the rationality of post-Newtonian science and in the ideas of the Enlightenment of the seventeenth and eighteenth centuries.

The key ideas of modernity which have shaped our Western culture – and beyond – have been a belief in science, reason, rationality, education and the inevitability of progress. In theory there were no problems which could not be solved by the onward march of science and technology; the spread of education and democracy would promote better relationships between individuals and nations; the new secular psychologies would lead to better self-understanding and therefore more rational judgements. One must not take a jaundiced view of the achievements of modernity, for they have been considerable, and there are few people who would wish to put back the clock to 'premodern' times. The postmodern thesis is, however, that all this is changing, that we are now living at a time of major cultural transformation. Among the most fundamental changes which are alleged to be taking place are epistemological changes, changes in which we come to know the truth of things.

In *Faithful Change: The Personal and Public Challenges of Postmodern Life* (1996) James Fowler helpfully separates the concept of postmodern society from the abstract philosophical discussion of postmodernism. He points out that in the last two decades the term 'postmodern' has taken on three broad meanings:

1 It is used as a term – somewhat apocalyptic in tone – to designate the transitional line in history and culture in which we presently live.
2 It is used as an aesthetic descriptor, suggesting a type of contemporary art and representation that is permeated with material interest, commercial distortion, and self-conscious intent to reshape perceptions.
3 The term refers to a broad development in contemporary thought that engages in deep-going criticism of the Enlightenment, with its trust in the possibility of universal reason and its focus on metanarratives such as belief in human progress and universal groundings for ethics, principles and standards. (Fowler 1996, 15)

Fowler's concern (and mine) is predominantly with the third of these meanings, with the failure of Enlightenment philosophy to provide an adequate framework for understanding contemporary experience. While there is much philosophical debate about the nature of this cultural shift, Fowler makes a further important distinction:

whether or not the average person in today's societies has a *theory* of postmodern experience or not, we are – *willy nilly* – finding ourselves living in and developing forms of *practical postmodern consciousness*. (Fowler 1996, 15)

Thus Fowler's focus is not upon abstruse academic theory but upon the ways in which people understand and describe their lived experience. He has identified some of the factors which shape our understanding of the world in which we live, the postmodern consciousness. These include:

- instantaneous communication bringing the world into our living rooms;
- experiencing the impact of global systems of economic interdependence;
- the resurgence of interest in particular cultural traditions and the juxtaposition of racial and ethnic conflict;
- the growing realization of ecological interdependence and the fragility of the earth's biosphere;
- the transition from heavy industries to service industries;
- the dominance of the electronic chip in all spheres of life;
- the end of the world of Cartesian philosophy and the increasing influence of theories of relativity, indeterminacy and chaos.

All of the above point to a context for ministry which has changed profoundly within one generation. The advent of postmodernity has involved transformations within society, within moral values and within religion itself, which all are significant for pastoral practice.

THE SOCIAL CONTEXT OF MINISTRY

The postmodern social context of ministry is characterized by rapid change. It is trite to point out that social change is on-going. What is characteristic of the present time is the speed at which change is taking place. An interesting thesis could be written seeking to correlate social change with technological change. Certainly there is much *prima facie* evidence that this is the case. The world of work is at least for many people dominated by new technology. We are witnessing the decline of heavy manufacturing industry and the rise of the service industries. There are now few jobs for which computer literacy is not essential or at least desirable. For many people, even the eminently employable, a job for life is a thing of the past. The need for constant retraining, of life-long learning, is a fact of life. And for those who are incapable of developing new skills there is the prospect of only very poor jobs, or worse still, no job at all and membership of a dependency sub-culture. New tools which empower some disenfranchise others. The gap between affluence and poverty is not diminishing. The signs of both affluence and poverty are not hard to find. New supermarkets, temples of a rampant consumerism, seem to open up with a rapidity which makes one wonder where the money exists to support them all. 'Homo Tesco' is alive and well. At the same time homeless men and women sit in the streets of our cities, begging for the crumbs from our tables.

This period of rapid change is also accompanied by an information explosion. There is little which is secret that remains hidden. Within a generation, flickering black-and-white, one-channel television has developed into a multi-channel communications system involving satellite and cable bringing a never-ceasing multitude of images from around the world into our homes. We no longer simply watch 'the news'; sometimes by watching events as they happen we become part of it. Information and entertainment, debates and disasters, politics and pornography all become part of that world in which we (and our children) live and move and have our being. We cannot escape from the 'news of the world' except by becoming hermits in the wilderness. The consequence is that we are all now much better informed (or mis-informed) about what is going on in the world. Yet it is almost certain that we are only at the beginning of a process in which all the contemporary modes of communication – television, personal computers, the internet and the mobile phone – become part of one vast network driven, at least partly, by advertising and consumerism.

The spirit of postmodernity is well summed up by Zygmunt Bauman in an image drawn straight from the communications revolution:

One may say that if the 'media which was the message' of modernity was the photographic paper (think of the relentlessly swelling family albums, tracing page by yellowing page the slow accretion of irreversible and non-erasable identity-yielding events), the ultimate postmodern medium is the video-tape (eminently erasable and re-usable, calculated not to hold anything forever, admitting today's events solely on condition of erasing yesterday's ones, oozing the message of universal 'until-further-noticedness' of everything deemed worthy of recording). The main identity-bound anxiety of modern times was the worry about durability; it is the concern with commitment-avoidance today. Modernity built in steel and concrete; postmodernity in biodegradable plastic. (Bauman 1995, 81)

To reflect upon the changes which took place within the twentieth century makes it virtually impossible to imagine the world of 2100 and beyond. This is the postmodern world in which ministry must be exercised. It can be a world of profound anxiety. If instantaneous communication may render a nuclear attack less likely, the threat of nuclear accident or ecological catastrophe is real for many people. Whether the general public really has any understanding of genetic engineering is open to question. What is not is a widespread anxiety about 'Frankenstein foods', driven not by knowledge but by ignorance. If there is a decreasing tendency for people to look to religion as a source of meaning and value, the fate of 'science' is little better. An optimistic assessment of the philosophies and practical benefits of modern science, prevalent at the beginning of the twentieth century, has given way to more realistic, if not more cynical, attitudes at its end. The 'grand narrative' of science no longer holds sway. The very rapidity of social change, driven by science and technology, makes it difficult for many people to adjust to its consequences before that new accommodation is itself obsolete. If, however, the social context of ministry has changed, so has its ethical context.

THE ETHICAL CONTEXT OF MINISTRY

The postmodern ethical context of ministry is characterized by moral relativism. There has been a tendency on the part of moralists to bemoan the fact that 'things ain't what they used to be'. This is certainly not my purpose. Rather, I wish to draw attention to the rapidly changing moral landscape in which ministry must be exercised and to do so as fairly as it can be done from the perspective of one individual. Again it can be argued that technology has set the agenda particularly in two important areas of debate within the public domain, namely bioethics and human sexual ethics. Not only has the new technology itself raised profound ethical issues unimagined a generation ago, but technologically driven mass means of communication, particularly television, have brought these issues into sharp public awareness. Assisted reproduction, organ transplantation, life-support systems, the setting of priorities and matters of resource allocation, the human genome project and related issues of communication and confidentiality – to list only a selection of current issues in medicine – all raise complex ethical issues. These are debated at a number of levels from the sophisticated argument of the academic philosophers to the *ad hominem*, but deeply felt, perspectives of those who have been influenced by television (either news or documentary) or more sharply through personal or family involvement. Certainly my 15 years of experience as chaplain in a large teaching hospital taught me that there could be no effective pastoral ministry without an awareness of the impact of technological advance upon patients, their families and hospital staff.

- In what circumstances was it appropriate to ask for the organs of a young man brain-dead as the result of a traffic accident?
- At what point should patients be deemed 'not for resuscitation'? Who should decide?
- How many resources should be directed towards a programme of assisted reproduction (at the expense of some other worthy project)? Is childlessness a disease?
- Should a very large sum of money be spent on treating a child when that treatment will almost certainly be futile?

While these are issues which confront hospital chaplains on a daily basis, there are few parochial ministers who will not at some time be giving support to families (or hospital staff) in their congregations who have to cope with their harsh reality. There are no commonly agreed answers to any of the above questions. Much will depend upon the perspective of an individual involvement. In the first case, a young mother waiting for a kidney may have a different perspective from the parents of the 'dead' man who may feel 'he has suffered enough'. In the second case, the family of an old man dying of cancer may feel 'while there is life there is hope'; hospital staff may feel he should be spared futile suffering. A childless couple may be experiencing acute personal distress because of their inability to have a baby; a Health Trust may wish to cut down their waiting list for operations. The family of a very sick child may feel there is no limit to what should be spent on their child; again, the Trust may be aware that the same sum of money could be spent effectively elsewhere. In such circumstances pastoral ministry will not consist of providing easy answers but of supporting people in the midst of a complicated and often distressing process of decision-making and of helping them to live (and sometimes die) with the consequences of the decisions taken.

It is, however, the area of human sexual ethics that has seen some of the sharpest debate and an apparent cultural shift towards a kind of moral relativism. There has sometimes been a tendency to equate ethics in general with sexual ethics. It was partly for this reason that I chose to deal with issues in medical ethics before issues in sexuality. Furthermore, there are other contemporary ethical issues to which our response is coloured by our personal perspective but which perhaps need to be considered within a broader framework. Our understanding of issues relating to wealth and poverty or crime and punishment or gender bias or the ab/use of the environment is inevitably perspectival, but it is possible that decisions taken in these areas will have more long-term implications for the good of humankind than those taken in the area of personal sexual morality.

Nevertheless, in the context of everyday pastoral practice, changing attitudes to sexual morality are profoundly important. Again, it is arguable that the trigger, if not the cause, of this change has been new technology, in this case the advent of the contraceptive pill in the mid-1960s giving women control over their reproductive capacity and a consequent sexual freedom equal to that of men. The title of a book by David Lodge, *How Far Can You Go?*, sums up the attitudes to sexual relationships before the availability of effective contraception. It is the story of a group of Catholic university students as they come to terms with the drivenness of their sexuality dominated by the twin fears of God and unwanted pregnancy. It was a time when any form of pre- or extra-marital sexual activity was widely considered as sinful and pregnancy out of wedlock was not simply inconvenient but shameful. Abortion, illegal prior to 1967, was not an option. The change over 35 years has been profound, as we see in current television programmes like *Sex in the City* with its emphasis upon the recreational rather than the procreational function of human sexuality. Cohabitation prior (and often as an alternative) to marriage is now commonplace, if not the norm, and the word 'partner' has taken on a new meaning.

Ours is the age of Anthony Giddens' 'pure relationship' which 'is entered for its own sake, for what can be derived by each person' and so 'it can be terminated, more or less at will, by either partner at any particular point'; of 'confluent love' which 'jars with the "forever", "one-and-only" qualities of the romantic love complex' so that 'romance can no longer be equated with permanence'; of 'plastic sexuality', that is sexual enjoyment 'severed from its age-old integration with reproduction, kinship and the generations'. (Bauman 1995, 90)

This seismic shift in human sexual relationships has occurred right across the social spectrum. It is a reality which has had to be addressed and accepted by many middle-aged church members who lived through the *How Far Can You Go?* years but whose children live under a different set of sexual rules. The churches themselves have responded to this new situation, both the Church of England and the Church of Scotland producing reports which, if not unanimous, gave a creative response to the new situation. Bishop Richard Holloway of the Scottish Episcopal Church has suggested a way forward for the churches:

This does not mean that the Church should abdicate the area of ethical debate; but it does mean that it should engage in the debate on the same terms as anyone else who has a desire to help in the formation of a healthy society. This means abandoning some of its claims to special wisdom or authoritative knowledge in the complex field of human relations. Like all people of goodwill, it will want to assist in creating or maintaining social arrangements which will protect children and their parents from abuse, lovelessness and rejection. It has something to offer from its own moral tradition and from centuries of pastoral experience and the wisdom that results ... There has been a sexual revolution in Western society in the last half century. Much has been lost, but much has been gained. If there is less self-discipline, there is also less hypocrisy; if there is less long-term commitment, there is a deeper understanding of the reciprocal nature of good relationships. (Holloway 1997, 134)

The pastoral implications of this sexual revolution and of new patterns of family life and living together are far-reaching. The postmodern family unit is not that of the cornflakes packet. Only a minority of households consist of a father, mother and two school-age children. Even as early as 1991, only 24 per cent of households in Britain consisted of a married couple with dependent children, with 26 per cent of households consisting of people living alone (Muncie *et al.* 1995, 139). There are also many one-parent families as a result of marital break-up; there are many people living alone by either accident or choice; there are many households consisting of composite families from previous relationships. While marriages end, relationships do not, especially where children are involved, and pastoral ministry in such situations must take this into account, as we shall see in the case study in Chapter Seven.

I do not remember in my parish ministry any couple who came asking to be married giving me the same address. I do recall my surprise around 1980 when a divorced member of the hospital staff came with her cohabiting fiancé and asked for a marriage service. Now it happens almost as a matter of routine. There seem to be two contrasting reactions among ministers to such situations. I have known some of a more conservative disposition who take a strong moral stance, even asking such couples to repent of their sin and live apart for a while before he (usually he) will marry them. A more realistic and pastorally constructive approach is expressed by Robert Randall in an article entitled 'What Do You Say After They Say "We're Living Together"?' (1979). While this article dates back to a time when cohabitation was just beginning to be common, Randall's response is, I think, still valid. He suggests that two questions should be in the minister's mind. The first is 'Why now?' Why, at this point in time, after living together, do you wish to get married? What is called for is an exploration of the factors in the couple's life which prompt them to seek this deeper commitment to one another. The second question is 'Why me?' What does it mean to you to request a Christian marriage service? An exploration of the responses to these questions will enable the minister to address their request in a pastorally sensitive manner, perhaps helping them to get in touch with the hidden, deeper meaning behind their request. As I will indicate below, there is for many people a spirituality which is not totally congruent with orthodox credal Christianity. It is surely right, and probably at the end of the day more profoundly evangelical, to affirm this rather than to condemn out of hand.

One cannot omit from a discussion of contemporary sexual ethics the matter of homosexuality. The Church's traditional stance against homosexuality is well known and does not need repeating. There is now within the Church a spectrum of responses from total rejection to total acceptance. Alongside a conservative view which regards homosexuality as a matter of choice and inherently sinful, there exists a more gentle view which sees the homosexual condition as essentially 'given', though no agreement exists as to whether the causes are biological/genetic or psychological or social. What is certain is that the issue is capable of generating more heat than light, though this is not always the case. In Scotland (as in England) the issue came to a head most recently in a decision to repeal Section 28 of the Local Government Act of 1988. This section related to the alleged promotion of homosexuality in schools. For those in favour of repeal, the issue was the prevention of bullying of young people whose sexual orientation was gay; for those in favour of retention, the matter was the prevention of the advocacy of a homosexual lifestyle among young people. When this was debated at the Church of Scotland's General Assembly of 2000, on the Board of Social Responsibility supporting the more conservative position, the Assembly refused to move to a vote on the matter, accepting that there were differing views, deeply held, within the Church. Now the General Assembly of the Church of Scotland is not noted for sitting on the fence on any issue! The decision not to decide should have been interpreted as an expression of a mature toleration of diversity of opinion within the Church. In fact, the press lambasted the Church for its failure to give a clear lead, with headlines such as 'Kirk sits on fence'. No doubt if a vote had been taken the same papers would have led the next day with 'Kirk deeply split on Clause 28'.

Postmodern society is marked by moral relativism precisely because issues are complex and there are no easy answers. There are those both within and outside the Church who think otherwise. This was well expressed by Richard Holloway writing in *The Scotsman* on the day after the death of Robert Runcie, the former Archbishop of Canterbury (13 July 2000). Many gave credit to Runcie for having held the Church of England together during a time of profound social and moral change. Others criticized him for an apparent lack of strong leadership. Holloway reflects upon a question he is not infrequently asked.

'Why doesn't the Church give a lead?' my expensively tailored neighbour at dinner will ask me . . . Apart from nostalgia for an imagined past, this call for leadership is usually a plea for public figures to echo the opinions or prejudices of the pleader. And there is usually a lot of that kind of reassurance on offer from politicians and ecclesiastics, but it is not leadership.

In the midst of complexity and ethical ambiguity the pastoral task is not to provide easy answers or to lead people to believe that such answers exist (if indeed they ever did). Rather, the pastoral task is to 'hold' people in the midst of the complexity and ambiguity and to help them to catch a vision or to be grasped by a grace which is more profound than the easy answer. Effective pastoral ministry is a parable of the gospel pointing beyond itself to the God who sustains us and carries us forward in the midst of change. If, however, postmodern society is marked by moral relativism, it is characterized no less by deep contradictions within religion itself.

THE RELIGIOUS CONTEXT OF MINISTRY

The postmodern religious context of ministry is characterized by pluralism and diversity. Religion in postmodernity is marked by three trends which on the face of it appear quite contradictory. These are, first, the decline in membership of the main-line churches; second, the rise of fundamentalism in Christianity and in other religions; third, a resurgent interest in 'spirituality' both within and outside the Church.

It is easy to quote statistics which chart the numerical decline of mainstream churches – at least in Britain. The figures relating to my own Church of Scotland are no exception to the general rule, as shown below:

	1951	1991	1998
Total membership	1,273,027	770,217	641,340
Baptisms	43,492	16,741	11,562
Admission on profession of faith	38,114	8,477	3,833

It is interesting to note that decline in membership has not led to a reduction in financial giving, the total increasing year on year and indeed keeping ahead of inflation. One could also point to other signs and anecdotal evidence of vigour and vitality in the Kirk: still a ministry in every parish in Scotland; congregations supported by the national church in areas of acute social deprivation; lively congregations scattered across the land providing relevant worship and a sense of community; the Society, Religion and Technology Project pioneering ethical reflection on the boundaries of technological change; a Board of Social Responsibility still one of the largest providers of social care in Scotland, pioneering (again) work in new areas, e.g. among women with HIV/AIDS and sufferers from Alzheimer's disease. It is too simple, therefore, to extrapolate from the current decline in membership to some point in the future when the Church of Scotland will no longer exist. It is arguable that contraction from the outside inwards is matched by growth from the centre outwards. Undoubtedly there is no room for complacency, though there must be an awareness that a new kind of church is emerging which will require new patterns of ministry, a point to which I will return in Chapter Eight.

It is also widely recognized that in the contemporary religious scene, theological voices of a more conservative persuasion have become more strident. Within the Roman Catholic Church, much of what was promised by Vatican II failed to materialize. In particular, when the Papal Encyclical *Humanae Vitae* did appear in' 1968, it quite unexpectedly restated traditional Roman Catholic teaching on contraception, to the consternation of many priests and laity alike. Having been proclaimed with all the force of papal authority, it is arguable that, paradoxically, no single action has done more to undermine its authority and credibility among both Catholics and non-Catholics. Sadly, this trend within the Roman Church has been accentuated by the pronouncement in September 2000 of the Declaration *Dominus Iesus* that non-Christian religions are 'gravely deficient' and the criticism of the Church of England and other Christian bodies as 'defective'. Within Protestantism, there has been growing strength among conservative churches which take a more literal view with regard to the interpretation of Scripture. Despite Bultmann and his demythologizing project, it appears that there are many things which 'postmodern man' is quite prepared to believe, even when their possibility is denied by what is regarded as 'modern' science. It is a strange fact that at the end of this scientific century, in which technology has wrought such previously unimaginable change, those forms of religion and church life which prosper and grow are conservative in theology and/or charismatic in expression. It may well be related to the need for some kind of certainty or the 'lead' asked for by Richard Holloway's dinner companion. This movement, however, is not restricted to Christianity but is reflected in a broader phenomenon within other world religions, e.g. Islam, which has also seen a resurgence in fundamentalism.

The contemporary religious scene is further complicated by the emergence of a fresh interest in the nature of the human spiritual journey. Even amid the apparent death-throes of institutional religion, there is on the part of humankind a searching for 'otherness', for that which is beyond life in the midst of life. General bookstores have shelves full of books on 'Mind and Spirit'; within the caring professions, particularly nursing, there is a concern to care for the whole person, particularly the 'spiritual' dimension, though the definition of the word 'spiritual' is seldom clearly defined other than to distance it from institutional Christianity. Interviewing potential students who wish to enter our Religious Studies programme could be a sad business. Not untypical was a young woman who wanted to be assured that she would not have to do any courses on Christianity. Buddhism or Hinduism was her preference. Exploration of the reasons for her choice revealed that her understanding of Christianity was a travesty of the truth and that her knowledge of the Eastern religions was virtually non-existent but nevertheless perceived as being a surer way to divine reality.

There is empirical evidence to support the existence of a spiritual search and experience which is non-institutional and non-Christian. The recent BBC Soul of Britain Survey shows that 76 per cent of the population admits to having a spiritual or religious experience, according to David Hay and Kate Hunt, a 59 per cent rise on a decade ago, though this may simply reflect a greater willingness to talk about spiritual experience. Nevertheless, commenting on the figures in the light of their own research at the Centre for the Study of Human Relations in Nottingham, Hay and Hunt write:

> We know, from the research we have done, that most people's spirituality is a long way from institutional religion. This spirituality has little doctrinal content, and few people have more than the vaguest remnants of religious language to express their experience of God. The phrase we commonly hear is 'I definitely believe in Something; there's Something there.' Their spirituality is based upon a longing for meaning. There is surely an echo in all this of St Augustine's famous phrase 'Our hearts are restless till they find their rest in Thee.' (Hay and Hunt 2000, 846)

An understanding of this contemporary, postmodern spirituality has implications for pastoral ministry. If the request for baptism is less frequent than it used to be, it still happens; if cohabitation is more common, couples still come to the church asking to be married; and if death has not gone out of fashion, 'secular' funerals are still a rarity. How much people really understand the meaning of these rites is open to question. Wesley Carr writes:

> The confusion of religious beliefs which are semi-articulated by someone who approaches the minister for a rite are unlikely to be so very different from the similar amalgam of belief which is held by the most committed church member. Ministers are dealing with the same phenomena of religion in different contexts of ministry. Because someone says a creed it does not mean that they either understand or believe what they are saying. When, therefore, ministers put heavy demands for understanding on those who approach them for, say, baptism, they need to reflect carefully on what they are doing. (Carr 1997, 210–11)

Carr treats this subject in the context of a discussion of what he calls 'common religion', sometimes also referred to as 'folk religion' or 'implicit religion'. He argues that this term holds together three things. First, while what is believed is not paramount, there may be beliefs which are deeply held but unarticulated. Even those who are able to express their faith in propositional terms may disagree about the meaning of the words – as we know only too well from a study of church history.

Second, people need rituals. In an earlier study on the 'occasional offices' (1985), Carr wrote of the connection between rituals and archetypes.

> When a body, such as the church, possesses powerfully specific symbols, which have an archetypal quality, then its behaviour, if not highly responsible, will be surprisingly damaging to individuals and society. (1985, 24)

People need symbols to mark the major transitions in life, such as marriage, the birth of a child, and death. These symbols help to meet deep archetypal needs. When the Church withdraws its symbols, even with rational explanation, there may be incomprehension and even disorientation because the archetypal needs are still there but unmet.

Third, Carr points out that such religion always retains some connection with the community. Increasingly, religion in postmodern times is privatized with an emphasis upon individual belief and perspective. The very fact, however, that a religious rite is sought points to a public dimension and an emphasis on human connectedness. Ministers are public figures representing public bodies and through their ritual functions help people to connect their individual and family stories with the story of the wider human community.

Some further comments by Hay and Hunt are relevant for pastoral practice in postmodern society:

> In these circumstances, the Church's major concern should not, in the first instance, be about filling pews. The first thing is to observe how God is already communicating with these many millions of people. They need to feel that even in a highly secular culture, there is still permission to develop the natural spirituality that is within them. The people we have been talking to in recent months tell us again and again that the Church is out of touch. This may be a wearisome platitude. But perhaps we should face up to the reality behind it. Perhaps the cliché is doing something more profound than simply accusing the Church of being out of date. Maybe it is telling us that we are not in touch with the ways in which God the Holy Spirit is already communicating with his secularised children. If the soul of Britain is waking up, perhaps it is time for us to take notice. (Hunt and Hay 2000, 846)

So far in this chapter I have sought to delineate the challenge of postmodernism by setting out some of the characteristics of the social, moral and religious context of the world in which we live. I have argued that we must take these challenges seriously. To take seriously these realities does not mean, however, to abandon our anchorage within the Christian story, and in due course I shall seek to explore the implications of that narrative for pastoral care. Before doing so, it is necessary to consider a second implication of postmodernism for such a theology of pastoral care, what has been called 'the eclipse of metanarrative'.

POSTMODERNISM, BIBLICAL TRUTH AND 'THE ECLIPSE OF METANARRATIVE'

'Simplifying to the extreme, I define *postmodernism* as incredulity towards metanarratives' (Lyotard 1984, xxiv). A basic tenet of postmodernism, encapsulated in the writing of one of the dominant proponents of the postmodern thesis, is that there is no universal standard of truth, no single story which has any significance other than a local one. This so-called eclipse of metanarrative, this demotion of the 'grand story', has obvious implications for the way in which Christians down through the ages, and in an amazing diversity of cultures, have appropriated the Christian narrative as having a profound significance for themselves both beyond first-century Palestine and beyond the boundaries of Western Christianity.

There are, however, theologians and biblical scholars who have sought to engage constructively with this postmodern critique of metanarrative, particularly as it relates to the importance of the Christian story for Christian belief and conduct, and to these we now turn. It is perhaps worth noting that some of the most interesting theological engagements with postmodern culture come from conservative evangelical sources (Dockery 1995; Sampson, Samuel and Sugden 1994). This may be understandable in light of the place which the biblical narrative has within this part of the Christian family – or at least is perceived to have – and the need to defend the biblical narrative from postmodernism's apparently corrosive critique of the importance of that narrative. If, however, we ourselves wish to make the Christian story central to a theology of pastoral care, we too must take seriously this same critique. In the remainder of this chapter we shall first examine the work of Richard Middleton and Brian Walsh, two Canadians who have sought to demonstrate that the postmodern critique of metanarrative is not as crippling as some have claimed it to be. Then we shall look at some of the insights of Walter Brueggemann (1991), the American Old Testament scholar, particularly as they relate to pastoral ministry. We have already noted the recent work of the American pastoral theologian Charles Gerkin, who postulates an understanding of pastoral care which 'stands between' the story of the Christian community and its tradition and the particularity of the life stories of individuals. Building upon the work of these scholars, we shall then in the next chapter proceed to explore the implications for pastoral care of dominant themes in the biblical narrative.

A DEFENCE OF BIBLICAL FAITH IN A POSTMODERN AGE

The fundamental issue is, of course, the normative, formative and indeed transformative nature of the Christian story. In their book *Truth Is Stranger Than It Used To Be* (1995), subtitled *Biblical Faith in a Postmodern Age*, Middleton and Walsh point out that from a postmodern perspective there are two central problems with metanarrative. The first is epistemological. If a narrative claims to be not just a local story but a universal story, a grand narrative encompassing world history from beginning to end, then far more is being claimed for it than is possible. It is generally agreed or at least argued that most metanarratives are social constructions, i.e. that they are products of a given culture. This being so, the problem with any metanarrative is that, in claiming universality, it is blind to its own constructed character and finds it difficult to encompass the rich diversity of lived human experience. The second problem with metanarrative follows from the first and is ethical. Since a metanarrative encompassing the universality of human experience is simply not possible, then metanarratives tend to legitimate the existing power structure and to trivialize, marginalize or suppress those whose stories and experiences do not fit the metanarrative. They are therefore oppressive.

What response is possible to this incredulity towards metanarratives? It must undoubtedly be taken seriously. It has to be recognized that many metanarratives have functioned ideologically, imposing their view of reality and suppressing minority stories in the process; and there has to be sympathy towards the postmodern case for affirming the importance of the proliferation of little, local stories. Christians must listen to others and learn from them.

But there is more to be said. First of all it is not only metanarratives which can be the source of violence, and the authors point out certain situations where the collapse of metanarrative has in fact precipitated the outbreak of even greater violence based upon local narratives. They quote Bosnia, Rwanda and Palestine as obvious examples where horrendous violence has been precipitated by local narratives (and we might want to add Northern Ireland to this sad list). Middleton and Walsh argue that humans need metanarratives and that even local narratives pertaining initially to a small community or tribe take on the status of universal narratives.

Second, they point out that the postmodern thesis itself takes on the status of a metanarrative though this is surreptitiously introduced and remains implicit. We are asked to believe that society has moved on from modernity to postmodernity, and within this story of societal development there is the implicit assumption that this is a good thing. In using the metaphor of the postmodern smorgasbord with a multiplicity of worldviews offered for our consumption, they argue as follows:

> If among the multiplicity of offerings we find Western modernist soup, Marxist rice, Christian stew and Muslim bread (so to speak) is there also a postmodern dish of some sort? Do postmodernists consider their own worldview as simply one option among many? Not at all. Postmodernity, as the master discourse which guides our understanding that all stories are merely human constructs, does not appear on the table. It is the table on which all the other dishes are served. Postmodernity thus functions as the larger interpretive frame that relativizes all other worldviews as simply local stories with no claim to reality or universality. (Middleton and Walsh 1995, 76)

But, argue our two authors, this is no reason to fault postmodernists since it is rooted in the valid human need for a worldview. We all need our big stories – even if it is postmodernism!

Middleton and Walsh argue a third important point in relation to metanarrative based upon the writing of the French postmodern philosopher Jacques Derrida. In a famous essay 'Plato's Pharmacy', Derrida comments on the complexity of the recurring term *pharmakon* ('drug') which Socrates applies to writing and which can have either a positive or negative meaning, whether it is a good thing or not. Derrida comments:

> This *pharmakon*, this medicine, this philter, which acts as both remedy and poison, already introduces itself into the body of the discourse with all its ambivalence. This charm, this spellbinding virtue, this power of fascination, can be – alternately or simultaneously – beneficent or maleficent. (Middleton and Walsh 1995, 79)

Middleton and Walsh sum up this part of their argument as follows:

> But even if tribal narratives may do violence and postmodernity tries to sneak in a metanarrative by the back door, perhaps the problem isn't metanarratives per se. Perhaps metanarratives, as we suggested, are *pharmacological* (both poison and remedy), harboring the potential for both oppression and justice, violence and healing. The important question,

then, would not be *whether* the Christian faith is rooted in a metanarrative, but *what sort of* narrative the Scripture contains. (Middleton and Walsh 1995, 79)

The contribution of Middleton and Walsh to my argument is therefore in the area of ground-clearing. They help us to see that the postmodern critique of metanarrative has its limitations. Further, more important than the existence of metanarratives and their influence is the way in which these metanarratives actually function. Do they bring good or evil? Are they therapeutic or harmful, salvific or destructive? That being so, we turn to the constructive engagement with postmodernism which we find in the work of Walter Brueggemann.

THE POSTMODERN–BIBLICAL–PASTORAL THEOLOGY OF WALTER BRUEGGEMANN

Walter Brueggemann, Professor of Old Testament at Columbia Theological Seminary in Atlanta, is doubly unique among biblical scholars. A teacher of theology within the Reformed tradition, he engages in constructive dialogue with postmodernism, using some of its insights to set Scripture free to speak in fresh and illuminating ways. And as a biblical scholar he is a frequent speaker at conferences of pastoral care specialists. Wherein lies his appeal?

Brueggemann embraces the postmodern tenet that much of our knowing is contextual and perspectival, that our attitudes and opinions depend to a large extent upon the place where we stand. In *The Bible and Postmodern Imagination* he writes:

> We are now able to see that what has passed for objective universal knowledge has in fact been the interested claim of the dominant voices who were able to pose their view and to gain either assent or docile acceptance from those whose interest the claim did not serve. (Brueggemann 1993, 19)

Because our knowing is perspectival, there can be no absolute certainty. It has to be accepted, asserts Brueggemann, that all our knowing is contextual, local and pluralistic. In such a situation, the use and development of the imagination becomes a primary way of knowing.

By imagination, I mean very simply the human capacity to picture, portray, receive, and practice the world in ways other than it appears to be at first glance when examined through a dominant, habitual, unexamined lens. (Brueggemann 1993, 19)

Drawing upon various theories of the imagination, Brueggemann argues that Christian preaching and proclamation are essentially an enterprise of imagining the world through the rhetoric of the text. He argues that we must allow texts to speak for themselves. For him, the crisis of modernity and postmodernity, the shift from hegemony to perspective, poses questions for the ministry of the Church.

Have we ourselves enough nerve, freedom and energy to move beyond the matrix of modernity and its confident, uncritical wholeness to trust the concreteness of the text?

Have we enough confidence in the biblical text to let it be our fund for counterimagination?

A no to these questions, in my judgement, consigns the church to disappear with the rest of modernity. A yes can be liberating for the church as a transformational model, liberating even for its ministers who must stand up and imagine. (Brueggemann 1993, 25)

For Brueggemann, it is the biblical text itself which 'funds' the human imagination, imagination being the 'quintessential human act', providing the pieces out of which a new world can be configured.

In an earlier paper delivered to pastoral care supervisors, 'The Transformative Agenda of the Pastoral Office' (1991), Brueggemann explores resources in biblical faith for a practice of pastoral care that is distinct from and critical of dominant notions of health in our society, providing an intentionally biblical rootage for pastoral care which offers a powerful alternative to the mode of health offered by our culture. Five claims of biblical faith are identified as being significant for health and therefore for pastoral care. First, 'God's reality is the source of health'. The basic assumption is that an autonomous self which lives from self and towards self cannot be healthy, reflecting an insight articulated by Calvin that right knowledge of the self and right knowledge of God are inextricably bound together. He claims that pastoral care in our culture is tempted to equate the transformative

promise of the gospel with a practice of stoicism whose characteristics are coping, adapting and enduring without reference to
matters of transcendence, holiness and mystery.

> Our theological work is to find ways of articulating this other
> One who initiates a relation and conversation of life and
> health. The responsibility to identify idols and articulate the
> true God who gives life should energize and summon those in
> pastoral care to more serious reflection on the narrative mem-
> ories of Israel and the church which disclose to us the truth of
> God. It is precisely in these narrative memories that the God
> who initiates health-giving transactions is primarily available.
> (Brueggemann 1991, 165)

For Brueggemann the 'truth' of the biblical narrative is central
for pastoral care. Other important themes are 'the centrality of
call' reflected in praise, obedience and mission; 'the neighbour
as the indispensable Other' giving rise to the mandate to care;
and 'the reality of sin and the possibility of forgiveness'. It is
these themes which constitute the identity and normative
tradition of pastoral care. They are themes which render it inherently subversive because they clash with the dominant ideology
of modernity.

> In that clash there is much at stake economically, politically,
> socially and morally. The subversive mandate of a biblically
> formed pastoral care goes hand in hand with a practical judge-
> ment that certain categories and questions can no longer be
> bracketed out. It insists on the reality of the transformative
> God, the centrality of call, the cruciality of neighbour, the
> reality of evil and the possibility of forgiveness, and participa-
> tion in a larger community, not because they are treasured
> ideas of a religious tradition, but because they are true. Health
> defined apart from them is false and is in fact a mode of death.
> (Brueggemann 1991, 174)

But how does the biblical narrative exercise its subversive power?
By what mechanism does biblically informed pastoral care
become transformative in the human situation? As previously
indicated, fundamental to Brueggemann's argument is his
emphasis upon the place of imagination. It is the telling of the
Christian story and the celebration of liturgy which provide
the material which 'funds' the imagination and which enables

pastoral care to be transformative of human lives. Indeed, for Brueggemann there is a close relationship between the pastoral and the liturgical. For him, 'Pastoral care is essentially a liturgical enterprise.' He identifies the conventional rituals of the modern, counselling-led pastoral care movement, such as intake interviews and the negotiation of fees, and, in contrast, advocates 'an *alternative liturgy* that will mediate alternative imagination, which in turn will yield different notions of health and wholeness'. He argues that those who receive pastoral care should be encouraged (indeed required) to participate in the regular liturgical activity of the pastoral care community.

> The theological ground for such a practice is that health does not emerge out of the immobilized parishioner or out of the wits of the pastor, but out of the memory of the tradition that has long mediated life and health to this community . . . The liturgic act intrudes a 'third voice' into the pastoral conversation – the voice of the Gospel. (Brueggemann 1991, 178)

What Brueggemann describes as an 'alternative liturgy' appears to be little different from the traditional ordinances of the Church, whether they be the sacraments or occasional offices such as funerals. A parish minister recounts the following story in which many of these themes are evident. In this case the 'alternative liturgy' is a funeral service following upon a particularly tragic death in the parish.

> I conducted the funeral of a 37-year-old woman who was brutally murdered outside her own front door in front of her two children (aged 10 and three). Her ex-husband committed the murder (and was later sent to prison). He had battered her throughout their marriage and she finally left when he began to sexually abuse their three-year-old daughter. She stayed in various hostels before moving back into the house where he finally found her. He waited outside all day, receiving cups of coffee from neighbours. When she arrived, he stabbed her about 20 times.
>   When I went to see her parents, who lived in the parish but were not members of the congregation, they asked if the funeral could be held in church (an unusual thing to happen in Scottish cities, particularly when the deceased is not deeply involved in the life of the church). They said to

me that they felt a huge sense of evil because of the way in which their daughter had died and that if they were to have a service in the church it might take away something of the sin. (Sin was their word, not mine.) They said to me afterwards that the service in the church was important for them. I have often thought about this since and am not completely sure of the exact nature of their request, but it seems to me to be an example of something which only the Church could provide.

So much is left unsaid or understated in this moving story. Left unsaid is the fact of pastoral initiative. There was trouble in a home in the parish, and the minister visited even though the folk were not members of the congregation. We do not know whether or not this family was known to the minister, but the minister was certainly known to them because of her reputation for her caring ministry in the community. From their experience of her at 'parish' weddings and funerals, the parents had a pretty good idea of how she would respond to their request to have the funeral in church. What are not stated are the reasons for their desire to have a funeral in the church rather than the crematorium, but also left unsaid was the minister's intuitive grasp that the service in church was important to them. It was expressed as taking away something of the sin, which is perhaps an expression that there were aspects of the situation which were deeply and radically wrong. What are also understated, perhaps never fully articulated, are their reasons why the church service was important to them. Perhaps we find a clue within Brueggemann's understanding of the transformative power of the Christian story and liturgy. It is arguable that though people do not go to church much, they have not forgotten the story, its memory revived by attendance at other funerals. In times of tragedy people still reach out for the 23rd Psalm and for the One whose parting gift was the gift of peace. Maybe the desire to have the funeral in church, and to take their daughter's body back into what was perceived to be a holy place, was a way of seeking a cleansing from the evil which permeated the whole situation. And perhaps this is what they found in the familiar words of the funeral service, in the reading of Psalm and Epistle and Gospel, in the promise of presence and peace and resurrection. Perhaps the funeral service conducted by that minister in that church invoked within their imagination the possibility that the evil which had invaded their lives might in time lose its power over them. We do not know. All of this is speculation, or perhaps pastoral imagination. For we will understand little of what is going on in pastoral situations unless we give play to our imaginations, checking out the reality of our interpretations where this is possible and appropriate. And we will not respond well and creatively in pastoral care unless we allow various possible options to 'play' within our imaginations.

Before departing from this account of Brueggemann's work, it is worth noting that he has drawn suggestive parallels between a postmodern approach to the interpretation of texts and the psychotherapeutic process. The process of psychotherapy requires attention to be paid to specific details of the stories of people's lives. The therapist must not come with preconceived ideas about the client but must allow truth to emerge from the specificity of what is presented. So also, the postmodern exegete must pay attention to the detail of the text, not ignoring what does not fit.

> The parts of the Bible that 'do not fit' credal theology or relational criticism may turn out to be the most important . . . A good exegete, like a good therapist, will linger over precise wording, the odd incongruity, the repeated accent in order to notice what commonly remains unnoticed . . . (In the Bible) the liberating, healing work of the text is not in the grand themes but in the acts and utterances that are odd, isolated and embarrassing. (Brueggemann 1993, 60)

Brueggemann's espousal of the psychotherapeutic necessity to pay attention to the details of the story which do not fit it brings to mind one of the key concepts of Clinical Pastoral Education, namely the 'cross-grained' experience identified by Thomas Klink (1966). Helping students to work through the cross-grained experience, to grow personally and professionally through broadening one's horizons to incorporate the new and unfamiliar, is a key process in pastoral supervision. Perhaps here we have another way of understanding the situation of the 'inarticulate ordinand' with which I introduced Chapter Two. His previous experience led him to believe that his academic study would equip him to cope with the anxieties and uncertainties of the people he met in hospital. That the reality of sitting by a hospital bed 'cut across the grain' of his previous experience was the beginning of a deeper wisdom, which grew out of a realization that he had to allow the peculiar reality of that particular situation to speak to him, and of helping him to find a new way of doing theology.

In this chapter we have explored some implications of post-modernism for pastoral care. I have attempted a description of the kind of society which is the common experience of all of us. I have also described two responses to the postmodern critique of metanarrative. If the first, that of Middleton and Walsh, was largely defensive of the biblical tradition, it is arguable that Brueggemann is the more creative and constructive in arguing for the importance of biblical narrative as constituting the identity of a pastoral ministry relevant for postmodern society. In the next chapter we shall explore the importance for pastoral ministry of some central themes from the biblical narrative.

CHAPTER FIVE

Biblical Narrative and Pastoral Care

If we regard the events surrounding the life of Jesus as normative for the Church's understanding of pastoral care, there could be a temptation to look no further than the New Testament, or even the Gospels, as our only relevant source. This, in my view, would be mistaken, for a number of reasons. The first is related to the more general reason why Christians study the Hebrew Bible and call it 'the Old Testament', regarding it as part of their Scriptures. The Hebrew Bible is the cradle of the New Testament. Jesus was steeped in its thought and any attempt to understand his life outwith that context is seriously impoverished. The second reason why we cannot ignore the Old Testament is that, as a part of the Christian Bible, it has had a profound impact upon Western cultural thought. While the supposedly sophisticated of our own generation (if asked) might write off the Old Testament as irrelevant, it is arguable that the appropriation (or misappropriation) of its thought forms continues to influence their attitudes (of this more later). Third, the Hebrew Bible is not just part of the Christian Bible. It is in its own right the Scriptures of the Jewish people. There is within contemporary Judaism a thriving pastoral care movement, and its representatives have made significant contributions to the British pastoral care movement as well as to recent international conferences. At the 1997 European Conference held in Ripon, England, one of the papers was given by Gilal Dror, a lady rabbi and pastoral counsellor from Israel. Reflecting upon her pastoral practice in the light of the biblical story of Abraham, Sarah and Hagar and their children, she concluded:

> The combination of religion and counseling . . . has the poten-
> tial to help us find inner strength through connection with
> God, and to find peace through involvement with community.
> Just by being there, the pastoral counselor is able at times to
> convey God's blessing, understanding and support to a person's
> struggle. (Dror 1997, 10)

What took place in that conference was a mutually illuminating
encounter based upon the interpretation of text and case from
the perspective of different religious traditions, the kind of
encounter demanded by and made possible by the pluralistic
nature of postmodern society. We turn, therefore, to identify Old
Testament themes which may have significance for pastoral care.

PERSPECTIVES FROM THE HEBREW BIBLE

In seeking to identify in the Old Testament certain themes which
might be relevant for pastoral care, there is an inherent problem
which must at least be recognized. At the time when I was a
divinity student in the early 1960s, the movement known as
'biblical theology' had a dominant influence upon the interpretation of the Bible. In reaction against the liberal theologies
which characterized the earlier years of the century,

> those involved in the new movement emphasised the distinc-
> tive nature of biblical concepts as opposed to their connections
> with their cultures surrounding ancient Israel and the early
> church . . . Added to that was a conviction of the essential
> coherence of the Bible seen in terms of overarching and
> pervasive themes and concepts. (Houlden 1983, 69)

And so we read G. E. Wright's *God Who Acts* (1952), John Bright's
History of Israel (1960) and G. von Rad's *Old Testament Theology*
(1957), all stressing in their own way the unity of the Old
Testament around such themes as the activity of God in the
events behind the Scriptures or in such unifying themes as
'covenant'.

Biblical scholarship has moved on, however, and current thinking reflects an emphasis upon the diversity of Old Testament
writings rather than their unity (which may of course reflect the
more widespread pluralism of contemporary postmodernity). In
the article from which I have just quoted, Leslie Houlden draws

attention to a new perception of the theological value of the Bible as a literary entity (or collection of entities), as containing 'story' whose message is of value apart from the events which may lie behind it. This position is, of course, fully congruent with Walter Brueggemann's case for allowing each text to speak to us out of its particularity, neither trying to make every portion of the Bible fit into some grand conceptual framework, nor ignoring the bits that do not fit. The danger is that in taking a thorough-going pluralist, postmodern approach to the Bible, one misses certain ideas which, if they have done nothing else, have influenced the way we think and therefore shape the context of the community of faith in which pastoral care is practised. Gene Tucker (1990, 799) in the *Dictionary of Pastoral Care and Counseling* draws attention to the fact of diversity which exists within the Old Testament and Apocrypha with regard to both the theology and practice of care. He also, however, identifies some contemporary implications for pastoral care. While Tucker does not go along with the central affirmation of the older biblical theology that there are certain overarching themes ('grand narratives'?) which run through the Old Testament, he takes a more modest position regarding certain perspectives which he believes set parameters that contain the diversity of thought within the Old Testament. Among these basic perspectives are the following:

1 *The theocentric character of biblical thought.* Belief in a God who is active in human affairs is simply assumed, never argued about. Therefore the implicit context of the care of women and men for one another is always the greater care of God for his creatures, God's *hesed*, usually translated as 'loving kindness'.

2 *The covenant relationship.* Men and women are not simply part of the created order, they are also regarded as children of God destined to enter into a covenantal relationship with a heavenly Father. Promises of mutual faithfulness are entered into between God and his children. Yet their fulfilment from the human side is marked by ambivalence and ambiguity. On the one hand, as children of God, men and women have the capacity to choose life. On the other hand, 'human lives are characterized by finitude, sin and brokenness'.

3 *Biblical care is communal and corporate, not individualistic.* Humankind lives not only under covenant with God, we live

in covenant with one another. As we have already seen, this is a perspective which is often foreign to contemporary secular psychotherapy but which is integral to pastoral care. The health and peace of individuals cannot be separated from the health and peace of communities. While this insight has never been part of the philosophy of psychotherapies with an individualistic orientation, it has been fundamental to more recent developments in community psychiatry, and to the thinking of others who have seen the local congregation as having enormous potential to become an arena of forgiveness, healing and growth, e.g. E. Mansell Pattison (1972).

4 *Biblical care is neither abstract nor general nor merely 'spiritual'.* The concreteness of biblical thinking leads to practicality in pastoral care. It is care for the widow and orphan; it is welcome for the stranger; it is bread for the hungry; it is comfort for the bereaved; it is justice for the oppressed; it is mercy for the sinner. The Old Testament understanding of care is a healthy warning to any who would spiritualize pastoral care, seeking to make people feel better or more religious while neglecting to attend to basic needs. For this reason, if for no other, we must see as fundamental to pastoral care, and not as a secondary expression of it, the thousands of acts of human kindness which are integral to the health of congregations and communities.

5 *Biblical care encourages the full and free expression of feelings.* In the Old Testament, the relationship with God allows for the full expression of emotion, negative as well as positive. Even in prayer and worship, and nowhere more prominent than in the Psalms, we find expressed the full range of human emotion, sorrow intermingled with joy, despair alongside hope, and anger directed even towards God. So also in our pastoral care, people must feel free to be themselves, to be real. Rightly or wrongly, it is sometimes assumed that in a Christian context, the expression of only some feelings is acceptable. Politeness may come to be valued more than honesty and openness. The cult of niceness may do much to hinder pastoral ministry among those who have good reasons for needing to give vent to negative feelings which reflect previous bad experiences, especially when these have been related to church people or even what they believe to be the absence of divine love in their lives.

6 *Biblical care is characterized by diversity.* There is no single pattern of care in the Bible and there seems little evidence of specialized ministries of pastoral care. God's mercy was expressed in different ways in each generation, and it is futile to seek to identify what does not exist. But the prophets were concerned with justice and mercy, wise men cared through giving instruction and advice and priests conducted rituals which brought to mind the goodness of God in days gone by. A prototype for the person-centred counsellor cannot be found in the pages of the Old Testament. When Job's world fell apart, he needed someone to sit alongside him and listen; instead he was given a theological answer – and a bad one at that, for theodicy is seldom, if ever, an appropriate pastoral response to tragedy. What we have previously noted is that people participated in care for one another. Community appears to have been real and not, as I once heard it defined by a cynical psychiatrist, 'a collective noun signifying many but not signifying much'.

NEW TESTAMENT THEMES

I am sure I am not alone in being able to identify a small number of books which, once read, have left a near-indelible impression on one's thinking and a consequent impact on other areas of thought, some related and others not. Among my small number of 'core' books I would need to list Dietrich Bonhoeffer's *Ethics* (1955). I can still remember the excitement of first reading it. Its theological framework for Christian ethics seemed to hold together and clothe in words two criteria which I believed were essential for the Church's pastoral ministry. The first was that it should reflect the essence of the gospel; the second was that it should be a response to real human need. Two phrases from the *Ethics* proved to be a rich resource for further exploration. The first was 'conformation with Christ'; the second was 'correspondence with reality'. The rest of this chapter will be devoted to working out the implication of the first phrase for pastoral ministry.

First of all, however, it is worth noting in passing what Bonhoeffer meant by 'correspondence with reality'. Exploring the nature of responsible Christian action, he wrote:

The responsible man is dependent on the man who is concretely his neighbour in his concrete possibility. His conduct is
not established in advance, once and for all, that is to say, as a
matter of principle, but it arises with the given situation ...
For the responsible man the given situation is not simply the
material on which he is to impress his idea or his programme
by force, but this situation itself is drawn into the action and
shares in giving form to the deed. (Bonhoeffer 1955, 97)

For Bonhoeffer, Christian ethics had to take seriously the realities of a given situation. It was not possible to come with abstract
theological principles and 'apply' them. Christian ethical decision-making was not, however, simply (as we have noted before)
'servile conviction in the face of the fact' (Bonhoeffer 1955, 198),
i.e. Christian moral decisions must not be totally determined
by the realities of the situation. Nor was there 'a principle of
opposition to the factual', for 'both of these extremes were far
removed from the essence of the matter'. Thus the human situation has to be taken seriously in all its humanity and ambiguity,
without allowing a willingness for dialogue with the human
situation to degenerate into domination by that situation. The
transposition of this idea from ethical decision-making to pastoral care is not hard to make. Thus, pastoral care must be
informed by the insights of the human sciences, though it is
arguable that in its first fascinated engagement with the secular
psychologies and therapies what sometimes emerged was pastoral care's servile conviction in the face of the (psychological) fact
which, in turn, led to an amnesia about its biblical roots. Pastoral
care must also take account of the realities exposed by social
analysis. I do not argue for a postmodern pastoral theology. I
do argue for a theology of pastoral care which is relevant in a
society which is described as 'postmodern'. If contemporary society really is pluralistic, diverse, fragmented, with no core values
and dominated by the communications revolution, then this is
the context of the Church's pastoral ministry, whether it is
described as postmodern or anything else. 'Correspondence
with reality' is not, however, the only idea to shape Bonhoeffer's
Ethics. Of equal, or perhaps even more fundamental, importance
is his concept of 'conformation with Christ', and we now turn to
a consideration of the implications of this for pastoral care.

In introducing this idea into his theological ethics, Bonhoeffer
was very careful to distinguish it from other ways of thinking
about the place of Jesus Christ in the Christian life, such as those
which, like the liberal theologies which had dominated Christian

thinking in the nineteenth and early twentieth centuries, were embodied in an ethical code. These took the form of applying directly to the world the teaching of Jesus, or what were referred to as 'Christian principles' in accordance with which the world might be formed or reformed (Bonhoeffer 1955, 18). This approach had been found wanting. Two wars involving European nations supposedly influenced by Christian principles had left the world in a state of desolation and despair. Was another approach possible when attempts to apply the teaching of Jesus had failed so miserably? Bonhoeffer thought so.

> On the contrary, formation comes only by being drawn into the life of Jesus Christ. It comes only as formation in His likeness, as *conformation* with the unique form of Him who was made man, was crucified and rose again. This is not achieved by dint of efforts 'to become like Jesus', which is the way in which we usually interpret it. It is achieved only when the form of Jesus Christ itself works upon us in such a manner that it moulds our form in its own likeness (Gal. 4.19). It is not Christian men who shape the world with their ideas, but it is Christ who shapes men in conformity with Himself. (Bonhoeffer 1955, 18)

For Bonhoeffer, the Church is composed of those in whom Christ has taken form, not a religious community of those who worship Christ. This is what the New Testament means by the body of Christ. The Church has no independent existence apart from Christ, nor apart from the world, for 'the Church is nothing but a section of humanity in which Christ has really taken form'.

Again, I shall attempt to transpose to pastoral theology some of the ideas which are integral to Bonhoeffer's ethics. In particular we shall examine how understandings of the Christ-event, which we think of in terms of incarnation, crucifixion and resurrection, take form in and inform pastoral ministry. We shall see that Bonhoeffer's understanding of the Church is also important for pastoral ministry. For the Church cannot be a 'holy huddle', furtively isolating itself from the world. But rather, formed by Christ, it seeks to exercise a ministry of care in the world as part of a common humanity.

INCARNATION AND *AGAPE*

A central belief, perhaps *the* central belief, of traditional Christianity is that in the man Jesus, God, the 'something beyond', has become embodied in a human being. 'The Word became flesh and dwelt among us . . . full of grace and truth' is how this belief is affirmed in the Prologue to St John's Gospel. Later in that same Gospel, when the disciple Philip asks, 'Lord, show us the Father and we will be satisfied,' Jesus replies, 'He who has seen me has seen the Father' (John 14.8, 9, RSV). Leaving aside the issue of whether these were the exact words which Jesus uttered, the text itself points to the fact that the early Church certainly believed that in a very real sense the man Jesus was God in their midst, in itself a remarkable belief to hold in view of the radical monotheism of the Jewish culture into which Jesus was born. Many of the internal controversies of the first few Christian centuries raged around the relationship between the human and divine aspects of the person of Christ. What emerged from these controversies and became enshrined in the ancient creeds of the Church was the conviction that Jesus was both fully God and fully man, and that any deviation from belief in either the full humanity or the full divinity of his person was heresy. Yet, like confessions of faith, credal statements put an end neither to theological speculation nor to the search for personal understanding. In the liberal theologies of modernity we see a renewed emphasis upon the man Jesus and his teaching. Within postmodernism itself there are those who argue for its full compatibility with a theological position based upon belief in the incarnation. Writing in *Tomorrow Is Another Country*, Christopher Jones writes:

> It is in his particularity, and not in any abstraction from or denial of it, that Jesus of Nazareth becomes 'the Man for Others' and 'God for All'. For Christian faith, the ultimate truth and meaning of life is found not in a set of universal principles but in an individual person, situated in time and space and bounded by a particular set of principles, through whom the character and purpose of God is communicated. (Jones 1996, 22)

What are the implications of the incarnation for pastoral care? How does pastoral ministry conform to the coming of God among us? One implication of the incarnation is that the communication of Christian truth is relational and not propositional. The Word, the idea, the *logos*, became flesh and dwelt among us, full of grace and truth. What cannot be true, what must not be true, of pastoral care are the words of Edwin Muir, the Scottish poet, reflecting in his poem 'The Incarnate One' on the worst excesses of Calvinism: 'The Word made flesh ... is here made word again.' Words are important in pastoral care, saying the right thing at the right time. Sometimes, however, the absence of words is even more important, the active listening which allows a painful story to be told. Sometimes what is needed is a supportive silence that gives space in which the other can think the unthinkable before finding words to express what was previously inexpressible. Yet, while words are part of the stuff of normal human interaction, when words are spoken in pastoral conversation they will always arise out of the pastoral relationship. For pastoral carers whose identity is shaped by the Christian story, what we are in our pastoral relationships will always take precedence over what we say. The content of the pastoral conversation has its own importance, but only in the context of a pastoral relationship which embodies the grace and truth of the gospel.

The incarnation sheds light on the nature of the pastoral relationship in yet another way. The characteristics of any helping relationship are now well understood. The work of Carl Rogers (1961), confirmed by the research of his colleagues Truax and Carkuff (1967), has identified three core conditions necessary for any therapeutic relationship, conditions which transcend the theoretical orientation of the therapist. These are: genuineness or congruence; unconditional positive regard or non-possessive warmth or, more simply, acceptance; and accurate empathy. How far these are personality traits inherent within the character of the carer or simply skills which can be acquired by training (or a combination of both) is open for discussion. What can be argued is that an understanding of the incarnation helps us to see these conditions from a different perspective. The Christian God is One who identifies with and enters into the suffering of men and women. Empathy, therefore, the attempt to enter into the mindset of another human being, and the communication of that empathy, can be seen as something more than good counselling technique. It points to, and is an expression of, the God who in Jesus accommodated himself to us in the frailty of our humanity, and who in the midst of our frailty revealed his glory. Neither is acceptance simply an attitude of one person to another. For the acceptance inherent in the pastoral relationship is inherent in a deeper divine acceptance which lies at the heart of the God who is revealed in Jesus Christ. Underlying all pastoral ministry is the *agape* of God. Indeed, it is arguable that behind the acceptance which is at the heart of any therapeutic relationship is this same divine *agape*, for no one can truly accept and value another who has not experienced acceptance and a sense of self-worth at a deeply personal level.

CRUCIFIXION AND SUFFERING

'Born of the Virgin Mary, suffered under Pontius Pilate'. In the Apostles' Creed it is as if nothing important happened between the birth of Jesus and his death. To be sure, the four Gospels tell us much about the life of Jesus, though perhaps not as much as we would like. We read about his ministry of healing and find there a rationale for the concern for healing and wholeness which is integral to pastoral care. We read and re-read his parabolic teachings and continue to be surprised by the way in which they challenge our preconceptions. Yet the events which surround the ending of his life constitute a third of the text of the Gospels, emphasizing the 'cruciality' of his death. The cross is itself the most pervasive and enduring symbol of Christianity, whether worn discreetly as a piece of costume jewellery or standing massively in a great cathedral, whether displayed as a crucifix or empty as a sign of resurrection.

The death of Jesus, with its unfairness and its awfulness, is the embodiment of realities in the human condition to which symbols can only point imperfectly. The cross is a reminder that human nature can be exceedingly destructive, both of the self and of others. Modern examples abound, perhaps the most harrowing example being the Jewish Holocaust. An analysis of the reasons why people are admitted to hospital would reveal that a high percentage were there because of their lifestyle. Smoking, the abuse of alcohol and obesity contribute in no small measure to ill-health. In human relationships people engage in mutually destructive behaviour. While the language of sin can detract from an accurate description of the causes of human suffering, to eliminate the factor of personal responsibility is to leave us with a less than adequate understanding of why people suffer. Modern psychology has been a powerful tool in helping people to understand why they behave in certain destructive ways, and it is sometimes true that 'to understand all is to forgive all'. But it is also sometimes true that people come to feel a sense of responsibility for what has gone wrong in their lives or for what they imagine they have done to others. Sometimes the sense of guilt experienced is a realistic acceptance of responsibility; sometimes it is out of all proportion to the reality of the situation. The pastoral response to a sense of guilt requires great sensitivity.

There are brands of Christianity with an in-built tendency to play upon a sense of guilt, sometimes seeking to create one where none should exist, sometimes inducing guilt feelings out of all proportion to any wrong-doing. Yet there can also be a non-therapeutic move away from allowing people to take responsibility for their actions when these have had disastrous consequences. While this may be understandable in a mode of counselling which claims to be value-free, the possibility of owning responsibility and hearing a word of forgiveness is integral to pastoral care (Menninger 1973).

There are, of course, within the Christian tradition various theories about how forgiveness 'works', some of them rooted in the thought forms of a bygone age and, it seems to me, of limited helpfulness today. I do not find helpful the cruder versions of the theories of what is called 'penal substitutionary atonement'. These imply that an angry God needed to be propitiated because of human sin. Therefore he allowed Jesus to be crucified in order to satisfy his anger and, as a consequence, 'let us off'. I find more help in the idea that the One who was crucified was the One who became incarnate among us, and that the crucifixion was in itself the supreme declaration of the *agape* of God. In rejecting 'penal substitutionary' theories, I am not for one moment setting at nought the reality of human wickedness, of 'man's inhumanity to man'. The cross exposes this in all its stark reality. Yet because the crucified One is the crucified God, to use the title of Moltmann's book (1974), the Church has always seen in the cross not the triumph of evil, but ultimately, in the cross *itself*, a sign of hope. Rodney Hunter and Murray Janson comment on the significance of this for pastoral counselling:

If he who is Lord could become obedient unto death (the cross), if human beings could be worth such an infinitely great ransom (1 Cor. 6.20), then no counselor can merely hear out his or her counselee, with clinical sensitivity, insight and empathy. No: each person, and each person's situation, must move him or her to action. After all, the cross has shown us the ghastly injustice that people (and their structures) can perpetrate in the lives of others, and can do so, moreover, with a semblance of law and righteousness, in the name of God using religion and piety as instruments.

But, further, the cross reveals that humanity's most dire need does not lie in external circumstances but in itself, and offers a place where counselor and counselee alike can be radically and finally redeemed from guilt and sin (1 John 2.2) and may become truly free (John 8.36). (Hunter and Janson 1990, 249)

The suffering and death of Christ have other implications for pastoral care. In his book *Rediscovering Pastoral Care*, Alastair Campbell has written of 'the language of wounds':

> Surprisingly, then, wounds, which seem at first frightening and nauseating, can also be 'open and beautiful'. For wounds reveal that fine boundary between living and dying, which makes life so precious and so revered . . . Yet we must beware of becoming morbidly, even sentimentally, preoccupied with blood, wounds and death, as though they of themselves were sources of healing . . . Wounds, and the vulnerability which they represent, lead to healing *only* when they have been uncovered and dealt with. (Campbell 1986, 40)

This quotation is taken from a chapter entitled 'The Wounded Healer', in which Campbell engages with a book of the title by the Dutch Catholic pastoral theologian, Henri Nouwen (1972). Both books are rich in ideas which fund the pastoral imagination. Both emphasize the need for mutuality in pastoral care, that ministry is not something 'done' by an invulnerable 'carer' who has never experienced suffering to someone vulnerable who has had more than their fair share of it. Nouwen's point is that only those who have experienced suffering of some kind can help others. It has to be recognized that many of the best pastoral carers have themselves come through some kind of trauma and that from their woundedness emerges a source of healing for others. It has equally to be recognized that amid much that is positive in the idea of the wounded healer, there is room for distortion and misunderstanding. In the first place, the fact that carers have come through trouble themselves must not lead to a simplistic sharing of experience ('I have been there and this is what helped me'). Further, as Campbell recognizes very clearly, those who would care for others can only do so when their own wounds have been dealt with. It is for this reason at least arguable that those who undertake pastoral work of any intensity should themselves undertake what is normal for those who engage in counselling or psychotherapy, namely a journey of self-discovery, whether through personal counselling or spiritual accompaniment.

Pastoral care which is informed by biblical narrative is one which cannot but be formed by an understanding of the cross. If in the crucifixion of Jesus we see human degradation, individual and corporate, exposed, then there is no aspect of human life which cannot be contained by a pastoral relationship undertaken in the light of the cross. The fact that the crucified One was also the incarnate One means, if nothing else, that because 'God was in Christ', the crucifixion was not an event from which God was absent, but one in which God was truly present and which in some mysterious way within the divine providence has brought healing to broken lives. It is interesting to note that the article from which the Hunter/Janson quotation comes is entitled 'Cross and Resurrection'. Of course, the story of the resurrection has its own place in the Christian narrative. Yet it is possible to move too quickly from cross to resurrection, as though it were only the resurrection which makes the cross 'all right'. There is a part of the Christian tradition, often best expressed by hymn writers, which sees healing flowing from the cross itself. (See, for example, Passiontide hymns such as 'We sing the praise of him who died' and 'In the cross of Christ I glory'.) To offer pastoral care in the light of the cross is to do so in a context in which human vulnerability and brokenness can be expressed, contained and transformed.

RESURRECTION AND LIFE

While we must not jump too quickly from cross to resurrection, the resurrection narratives stand gloriously as the climax of the earthly life of Jesus. It is futile to try to reconstruct 'what actually happened' at the resurrection. It was certainly not what David Jenkins, while Bishop of Durham, called 'a conjuring trick with bones'. What is real is the experience and conviction of those who were with Jesus in the flesh, and who witnessed his death, that he was alive. What is real is the transformation of a despairing, dejected group of people into a missionary band which in worship and life started a movement that sent the message of the Risen Christ to the ends of the earth. What is real is the experience of women and men down through the ages, whose lives have been changed by this belief. In a perceptive study of the resurrection in which he explores the relationship between narrative and belief, my colleague Ian McDonald demonstrates how a belief in the resurrection infuses every section of the New Testament. He also argues that we cannot study the resurrection narratives in the New Testament without being drawn into them. As we seek to interpret them, they interpret us – ideas which are congruent with the hermeneutical theories of Paul Ricoeur outlined in Chapter Three. McDonald writes:

> To interpret the resurrection is therefore a complex process. It involves a critical study of the source documents as well as an elucidation of the cultural context in which word and concept are used . . . But the process moves readers, inexorably, to consider their own finitude, and to view the new perspectives which resurrection opens up as live options for themselves. They are thus confronted with a new understanding of life and death, hope and despair, goal and purposelessness, the scope of 'bodily' existence and mortality. The perspective of resurrection, therefore, impinges on worldly or everyday existence, as it does in the story of Jesus 'in the flesh'. It evokes a power or dynamic which enables one to transcend the apparent hopelessness of a given human situation and to lay hold of the new creative possibilities of faith and hope. (McDonald 1989, 3)

These words of Ian McDonald are of direct relevance for pastoral ministry formed by Christian narrative. Let it not be thought that I am advocating that the theological ideas of which I am writing should be part of the content of pastoral conversation. I have already, in discussing the approach of Thurneysen, highlighted the limitations of pastoral care as proclamation. The great affirmations of the Christian must never be used as a kind of pastoral Elastoplast/Band-Aid/sticking plaster to cover up the deep wounds of the human soul. (Let it also be noted, however, that neither must their use be banned *a priori*, for it is sensitive exploration of a theme such as resurrection which may bring deep peace to someone who is hurting.) What the great themes of incarnation, suffering and resurrection contribute to the pastoral relationship is not content, but context.

The incarnation, God assuming our human nature, speaks of God *with us*; the crucifixion, God becoming vulnerable, speaks of God *for us*; the resurrection, death defeated, speaks of hope in the midst of despair, of life transcending death, of God *with us* and of the possibility of new beginnings. Whether or not these ideas are ever communicated verbally to the one being cared for, they shape the world of the one who claims to care for the other. That being so, the context of pastoral care is one in which, no matter the extent of the distress revealed, there is a presumption of God's power to bring healing and renewal.

SPIRIT AND PRESENCE

Incarnation, crucifixion, resurrection – these are words which Christians apply uniquely to the events surrounding the life of Jesus. The biblical narrative does not, however, end there. It goes on to speak of ascension and the coming of the Holy Spirit. Again, it is idle to speculate about 'what actually happened' and to try to understand these events in human terms. All that can be said for sure is that after some time the resurrection appearances of Jesus, as described in the Gospels, ceased; and that soon after, those who followed Jesus experienced the power of God among them in a new way. In the New Testament narrative, resurrection, ascension and the coming of the Spirit are inextricably bound together. During the resurrection appearances, Jesus told the disciples that he would go away, and that it was for their good that he should do so. We then have the strange story of the ascension. In Luke we are simply told, 'Then he led them out as far as Bethany, and blessed them with uplifted hand; and in the act of blessing he departed from them' (Luke 24.50, 51). At the beginning of Acts, Luke further elaborates this story, saying, 'he was lifted up before their very eyes, and a cloud took him from their sight' (Acts 1.9, 10, a story reminiscent of the departure of Elijah in 2 Kings 2.1–12) and this is followed by the story of the coming of the Spirit at Pentecost. In *The Living Reminder* (1977) Henri Nouwen links these events together in a way which is pastorally significant.

In our ministry of visitation – hospital visits and home visits – it is essential for patients and parishioners to experience that it is good for them, not only that we come but also that we leave. In this way the memory of our visit can become as important, if not more important, than the visit itself. I am deeply convinced that there is a ministry in which our leaving creates space for God's spirit and in which, by our absence, God can become present in a new way. There is an enormous difference between an absence after a visit and an absence which is the result of not coming at all. Without a coming there can be no leaving, and without a presence, absence is only emptiness, and not a way to greater intimacy with God through the Spirit. The words of Jesus: 'It is for your good that

I leave' should be part of every pastoral call we make. We have
to learn to leave so that the Spirit may come. (Nouwen 1977,
44)

I vividly remember an incident from the early months of my
parish ministry which I would have handled very differently had
I then been aware of these words of Nouwen. An elder in the
congregation became terminally ill and was being nursed at
home. Even in the few months I had been in the parish, I had
become close to the family. As the end drew near I spent a lot of
time with them and was prepared to sit with them during the
last few hours. In fact just after midnight (a full twelve hours
before the man died) they very kindly sent me home to the
manse. On reflection, I now see that my need to be there, to be a
'good minister', far exceeded their need or wish to have me
there. I would have been more effective, I think, if I had visited
in the evening, said a prayer – and left. In the early days of
ministry it is possible to become quite messianic, believing that
the presence of God in a situation depends on our being there.
Instead we should offer such pastoral ministry as seems appropriate, and then get out of the way, making room for the
Spirit – and giving a family space to be with one another.

ESCHATOLOGY AND HOPE

When persons who are experiencing problems and difficulties
seek assistance from a pastor, they are, in this very act, seeking
hope . . . When the pastor initiates contact with a person who
is in difficulty, the pastor, through this very gesture, offers
hope. (Capps 1995, 8)

For Donald Capps, it is the ability to offer hope which is a major
characteristic of pastoral care and counselling. It is debatable
how far this is true. It is arguable that the first of the two statements in the Capps quotation is equally true of the secular
therapist. Indeed, no one in difficulty would agree to see a therapist unless there was some hope of improvement. The second of
Capps' statements might be equally true of friendship, for the
gift of friendship may itself be an expression of hope.

What hope do pastors bring to their care for people? In certain
circumstances it is the same hope as the secular counsellor,
and that is hope based upon experience. Even in the acute
sense of despair that can follow a bereavement, both pastor and

counsellor know that grief is a process, that time is indeed a healer, and that most people eventually are able to begin to live again. It is not as though the death of a loved one is of no consequence but in due course, by becoming able to incorporate the loss into their lives, people move on, still themselves but changed by the experience. It is this knowledge based upon experience which allows pastors and counsellors to sustain the bereaved with a quiet confidence, to 'hold' them while the natural healing processes of the human psyche take their course.

There may also be a modest hope for both pastor and counsellor based upon their experience of the efficacy of the helping relationship. They know that the very provision of such a relationship of active listening, of non-judgemental acceptance, of affirmation of the other, is in itself a communication of hope. Because others (and as often as not they themselves) have benefited from such a relationship, carers trust that what has been effective in the past can also work again.

Within psychotherapy itself, the school which has laid most emphasis upon hope is rooted in the logotherapy of Viktor Frankl (1988). His experiences in a concentration camp confirmed a previously held suspicion regarding the importance of hope for human survival. The prisoners who survived were those who had something to which they could look forward, a hope to fund their 'will to meaning'.

Andrew Lester sees hope and the lack of it as central themes in pastoral care:

> For the pastoral care specialist this connection with future tense carries additional theological consequences having to do with hope and despair. When a future story is disturbed, then the hoping process is vulnerable to despair. Conversely, when hopelessness overwhelms a person then we know that something has happened to her or his future images. A future story has been lost, stolen, abused or distorted by a developmental snag, a traumatic event, or any combination of life forces. (Lester 1995, 44)

The task of the pastor is to help in the construction of hopeful future stories, of invoking within the imagination of someone in despair the possibility of seeing life differently. Lester, while suggesting some techniques to facilitate this process, offers no easy solutions and does not underestimate the problem of resistance. What is important theologically is that Lester locates the possibility of constructing a hopeful future squarely within a Christian understanding of hope.

> One goal of the pastoral relationship, therefore, is to guide persons infected with hopelessness in developing meaningful relationships with a community of hopers. The pastor represents God and the whole history of the Christian tradition – an identifiable community that projects itself into the future. Since hoping is a shared experience it has a contagious quality. People can 'catch' the atmosphere of hoping from the pastoral caregiver and the people of God with whom they get involved. (Lester 1995, 99)

In recent years there has been a revival of interest in 'the theology of hope' largely influenced by the work of the German theologian Jürgen Moltmann in a book of that title. According to Alister McGrath,

> Moltmann argued the need for the rediscovery of the corporate, Christian conception of hope, as a central motivating factor in the life and thought of the individual and the church. Eschatology needed to be rescued from its position as 'a harmless little chapter at the conclusion of a Christian dogmatics' (Karl Barth), and given pride of place. (McGrath 1994, 549)

The Christian hope is one that transcends a trust in the natural healing processes of the human psyche and a reliance upon 'what works' in therapy (though it is big enough to encompass both of these). The Christian hope is rooted in faith, in faith that when the Christian story has been told, a story with themes of preparation and incarnation, of crucifixion and resurrection, of ascension and the coming of the Spirit, even then the whole story has not been told. As the story has a beginning, even so it shall have an ending. We may only see 'through a glass darkly' but the distorted images which we do see reflect the ultimate victory of God, the overcoming of evil by good. They are images of healing and renewal, and of course we can only grasp them imaginatively and in faith. Yet a pastoral care which is 'conformed with Christ' must be conformed with the whole story. We are to show forth the Lord's death 'until he comes'. It is in this context that the pastoral relationship is able to 'hold' those who suffer, underpinned by the faith that the words and actions of pastoral care belong to what Bonhoeffer called the 'penultimate', and that beyond the penultimate there is another 'ultimate' word which at the end of the day brings healing and wholeness.

CHURCH AND WORLD

Meanwhile, the Church lives in the 'time between the times'. The coming of the Holy Spirit described in the beginning of Acts marks the beginning of the story of the Church and its expansion throughout the world. The story of the ascension signifies more than the end of the resurrection appearances. The story of the ascension, of Christ 'seated at the right hand of God', introduces the motif of Christ's Kingship and of the call to obedience. Those who follow Christ are to take the message of God's love to the ends of the earth. The commission is to preach the gospel and heal the sick. This has been done for two millennia. The outreach of the Church into the world has taken many forms. As the expansion of the early Church followed the roads of the old Roman Empire so has the Church spread in tandem with other developments in travel, colonization and communication. There have been elements of ambiguity in the missionary expansion of the Church and events in which the Church cannot take pride. On the whole, however, the spread of the gospel has brought in its wake significant developments for human well-being particularly in the areas of health and education. The Church's contemporary ministry of pastoral care is only one manifestation of this mission. Of course, it is unethical to set out to use pastoral care as a means of evangelism – and usually counterproductive. Yet there is nothing so profoundly evangelical as good pastoral care. This is the place where the gospel becomes an embodied response to human need and grace becomes incarnate.

Today, throughout the world, the message of the gospel finds expression in many forms: in worship and preaching; in education and teaching; in social service and in the provision of health care; in dialogue with those in the media who shape public opinion; and in pastoral care. Pastoral ministry is not the only ministry of the Church but it is an important one. In the remainder of the book we shall explore the shape and the content of this ministry in the context of postmodern society.

CHAPTER SIX

Faith Development and Pastoral Ministry

How can one minister faithfully in the midst of cultural diversity? What is the distinctive nature of a pastoral ministry 'funded by' the Christian story amid the competing ideologies of the postmodern world? In attempting to describe the kind of pastoral ministry which is now required I will draw upon some further work of James Fowler in which he relates earlier important work on what he calls 'stages of faith' to shifts in cultural consciousness.

FAITH DEVELOPMENT THEORY AND MINISTRY

We have already noted Fowler's definition of the new emerging discipline of practical theology, a definition which, I believe, sets the parameters for the kind of pastoral care which I am advocating is necessary for postmodern society. We have also drawn upon his distinction between the philosophical discussion concerning postmodernism and the 'practical postmodernism' which provides the matrix in which we live our lives.

Fowler is, however, best known for his contribution to our understanding of human development, in particular for his faith development theory. Other theorists have contributed to our knowledge of different aspects of human growth and development. Freud (1905) did seminal work on emotional and sexual development; Piaget (1950) proposed a model for cognitive development in children; Erickson (1965) introduced us to 'life cycle theory' with his 'Eight Ages of Man'; and Kohlberg (1976) has made a substantial contribution to our understanding of moral development. Fowler's distinctive contribution (1981) has been empirical research which has contributed significantly to our understanding of how people come to believe or have different kinds of faith. Based upon interviews of over 500 representative Americans, aged from four to 90, of different religious affiliations (and none), Fowler and his associates set out the seven stages that emerge as we work out the meaning of our lives. Fowler showed that all people move through the same stage sequence, despite the fact that the contents of their images, values and commitments may be quite different. Furthermore, he has shown that not many (indeed few) people complete all the stage sequences, but remain stuck on a plateau, providing at least some explanation of the fact that even people brought up within the same religious traditions may have very different understandings of what faith means and, conversely, that people brought up within very different religious traditions may share common attitudes to life.

Fowler's work has obvious implications for pastoral care as he himself has demonstrated in his *Faith Development and Pastoral Care* (1987) in which he works out the implications of his seven stages for pastoral care within the congregation. Of much greater significance, I believe, is his more recent *Faithful Change: The Personal and Public Challenges of Postmodern Life* (1996) in which he correlates three of his stages of faith development with what he calls the premodern, the modern and the postmodern consciousness. My thesis is that in this latest work Fowler points the way to an understanding of the kind of pastoral ministry called for in contemporary society. In the remainder of this chapter I will therefore summarize briefly Fowler's seven stages of faith; expand in more detail upon the three of these stages which Fowler correlates with certain developments in human consciousness; and explore the implications of Fowler's argument for the practice of ministry.

FOWLER'S STAGES OF FAITH

Fowler's research has identified seven 'structural–developmental' stages of faith which are summarized below. While, for the sake of completeness, all seven stages are listed, it is the fourth, fifth and sixth stages which are of particular significance for my argument. Fowler's stages are as follows:

1 *Primal faith.* This is characteristic of infancy, is pre-linguistic, and is formed within the matrix of the primary caring

relationships. Hopefully in this stage are sown the seeds of trust, self-worth and hope.

2 *Intuitive-projective faith.* Here the young child (aged 2–6) builds upon the acquisition of language and the awakening of imagination. Awareness of the deeds and perceptions of adults can awaken within children a capacity for attention to mystery and the numinous.

3 *Mythic-literal faith.* At this stage, typical of older children (aged 7–12), there is a firm grasp of cause and effect and the ability to test and change perceptions in the light of experience. Meaning is frequently found in narrative and story, though the interpretation of stories and beliefs tends to be literal and one-dimensional.

4 *Synthetic-conventional faith.* Closely related to the establishment of personal identity through interaction with others, this stage commonly takes place in adolescence (aged 12–17) and involves working at a set of unifying attitudes, beliefs and values which helps young people find support and a sense of who they are in relation to a peer group of similar beliefs and values. While stories and symbols may be seen as conveying different levels of meaning, they are not reflected upon in a critical way or related to one another. While this stage is typical of adolescence and finds its generation at this stage, Fowler argues that in fact many adults do not move beyond this stage in their faith development but remain 'stuck' in it.

5 *Individuative-reflective faith.* With the emergence of a more autonomous self, young adults (aged 17–35) progress to attitudes less dependent upon others and more upon a capacity for self-reflective awareness. The self is clearly differentiated from others with an emphasis upon autonomy and authenticity. Symbols, stories and rituals are all subject to questioning and their meanings capable of restatement in conceptual terms.

6 *Conjunctive faith.* Some adults in mid-life move beyond the previous stage, finding it inadequate to cope with their experience of reality. Truth is seen to be more complex, issues less clearly defined and a need is perceived to hold apparently contradictory views simultaneously, each of them essential to encompass the truth of things. There is a new 'epistemological humility' and the emergence of a more porous and receptive

stance towards the reality of others. There is also an 'avoidance of ideological over-confidence because of a heightened awareness of the degree to which the reality of Being exceeds the adequacy of all human effort to grasp it' (Fowler 1996, 65).

7 *Universalizing faith.* According to Fowler, this is a rare stage which few attain. It is characterized by a lack of concern for self and by a love of others grounded in the Being of God.

STAGES OF FAITH AND CULTURAL CONSCIOUSNESS

What is significant about Fowler's most recent writing is the way in which he correlates three of these stages of faith with the three different cultural epochs which he believes are important for understanding what is happening in contemporary society. Stage 4, synthetic–conventional faith, he correlates with the 'premodern' consciousness, i.e. with those attitudes, beliefs and values characteristic of the time prior to the Enlightenment of the seventeenth and eighteenth centuries. Stage 5, individuative–reflective faith, he sees as finding its fullest expression in the 'modern' consciousness, that cultural epoch which has existed from the Enlightenment until comparatively recent times, often considered to be the latter half of the twentieth century. In stage 6, conjunctive faith, Fowler finds parallels with the themes of postmodernity, some of which we have already identified.

Before setting out Fowler's argument in more detail, it is important to be clear about what he is not saying. He is not saying that every person in any particular historical epoch operated at the corresponding stage of faith. This is manifestly not true. In every historical epoch it is possible to identify individuals who have lived a life which can be described in terms of later stages of faith. Throughout the history of the Church, and indeed of the whole of humanity, it is possible to identify people, of many faiths and none, who have been people of integrity, confident in their own beliefs yet open to others, who have dared to think the unthinkable and push forward the boundaries of human understanding. Each of us might even want to identify our own 'stage 7 people', though few would dare to claim it for themselves (and any claim for oneself would surely be an automatic disqualification for its bestowal). Further, we have already noted Fowler's own observation that (for whatever reason) people can get stuck at any of the stages of faith and do not progress from (say) stage 4 to anything beyond. Herein, I believe, lies the importance of Fowler's work for pastoral care in postmodern times. In essence, it means that if we are to exercise a relevant ministry of pastoral care in contemporary society, we will need to learn to minister to people who are at different stages of faith in a world dominated by the values of postmodernity.

Fowler draws parallels between these three stages of faith and cultural consciousness. The first two he relates to the long-standing tension between the orthodox and progressive 'tempers'. These have existed in every society as well as being characteristic of the differences between societies before and after the Enlightenment. It is against the background of this tension that Fowler sets out his understanding of postmodern consciousness, which I will argue helps us to understand the kind of ministry required today.

SYNTHETIC–CONVENTIONAL FAITH AND THE ORTHODOX TEMPER (PREMODERN)

According to Fowler, the orthodox temper exhibits many of the structural features of the synthetic–conventional stage of faith and is closely related to pre-Enlightenment thinking. It is a worldview largely dependent upon an uncritical acceptance of external authority. Authority is located in sacred texts, in the tradition, in the group or in the group's authorized representatives. In religion, authority rests in a concrete and literal reading of the sacred texts, in the indisputable teachings of the tradition and the dictums of authorized interpreters. While good personal relationships may exist with individuals of different beliefs ('Some of my best friends are Catholics'), paradoxically this may prevent an examination of the differences which do exist. Negative stereotypes may be formed on the basis of difficult relationships with one representative of another group. I recall an elder in my congregation whose implacable opposition to all things ecumenical seemed to be based upon a bad experience with one Church of England chaplain while on military service 30 years previously. Unquestioned acceptance of their own religious tradition leads to an unexamined sense of its superiority and pressure to convert those of other traditions. There may be attempts to impose their own moral views upon the community through legislation, e.g. with regard to abortion and homosexuality. Premodern society can be described in organic terms with a cohesion based upon generally accepted values which encompass both private and public life. In both family and Church, patriarchal models are dominant. In society generally, authority is hierarchical, leadership controlling information as a means of holding on to power. Decisions are made by the few on behalf of the many on the basis of one-way consultation and communication.

INDIVIDUATIVE–REFLECTIVE FAITH AND
THE PROGRESSIVE TEMPER (MODERN)

The progressive temper is closely related to the values introduced in Western society by the Enlightenment and exhibits many of the features of the individuative–reflective stage of faith. There is a healthy suspicion of received tradition. Authority for decision-making is not located in external authority but within experience, reflective judgement and personal conscience, i.e. within the self. Reason and rationality are prized by progressive, modern thinkers. Opinions may change in the light of new evidence. The concept of demythologizing is an important feature of the religious consciousness. At this stage, myths, parables and symbols, and Scriptures are valued for their essential truth, but whatever is unacceptable to 'modern man' is filtered out or reinterpreted. Autonomous individuals freely and voluntarily enter into alignments with self-selected associations. There is a clear separation of private and public life, with what people do in private no concern of others providing no harm is done to others. Leadership roles are based upon meritocracy rather than aristocracy, with rational bureaucratic organization fitting in nicely with the progressives' predilection for contracts. Progressives value open debate and assert their confidence in the power of rational argument. In fact, says Fowler, an overconfidence in conscious rationality which is oblivious to unconscious distorting factors can lead to problems in organizations run along progressive lines. The debate, indeed conflict, between those of orthodox and progressive temperament is both long-standing and heated.

Much of this deeply conflicted debate in both Church and society generally has been carried on by representatives of the orthodox and progressive tempers, the arguments becoming 'stuck' and deeply divisive largely because the adherents of each position are constitutionally unable to understand where the

other side is coming from. Their own arguments seem so obvious, those of their opponents incomprehensible, either because
of an uncritical adherence to the traditions of the past or because
of an unprincipled compromise with the spirit of the age. Fowler
argues that at least some of the virulence with which the representatives of these two positions attack one another is rooted in
a realization, still only dimly comprehended, that both of these
positions are under siege from powerful forces shaping a radically new cultural and social consciousness which will dwarf the
impact of the Enlightenment. This is the phenomenon of postmodernism. As we have seen, Fowler has argued that whether or
not we understand the academic philosophical arguments, we
are all inevitably shaped by the new kind of society which is
emerging, the postmodern experience described in Chapter Four.
Fowler argues that there is a congruence between the postmodern
temper and the conjunctive stage of faith.

CONJUNCTIVE FAITH AND THE PRACTICAL POSTMODERN TEMPER

Fowler argues that the postmodern consciousness is dominated,
both implicitly and explicitly, by an awareness of systems thinking, and in this respect it parallels the conjunctive pattern of
faith consciousness. There is a need to hold together, in juxtaposition within one system, ideas, theories, realities which appear
(and often simply are) in conflict with one another. In the postmodern consciousness there are no pure 'facts'. All knowing
involves interpretation, and since people construct meaning
from their own particular perspective within a system, there can
be no approximation to 'truth' without taking into account these
different perspectives and interpretations, which are sometimes
mutually contradictory. Strangely enough, it is the recognition of
the multifaceted nature of truth which allows into the arena of
public consciousness a whole variety of different beliefs, even the
Christian gospel. Thus, accompanied by a kind of 'epistemological
humility' towards all beliefs, there is also a place for commitment in the midst of a pluralism of perspectives. Further, all
religious beliefs and worldviews require the creative engagement
of the human imagination. Organizationally, geographical factors
become (at least allegedly) less significant with new and immediate means of communication on a global scale. The resident
expert gives way to the temporary consultant. Relationships are
functional and less permanent.

PASTORAL MINISTRY AND STAGES OF FAITH

Recently I was involved in two very different conversations on the same day. Mrs A, a senior member of the university, berated me: 'What are you teaching these young ministers nowadays? Our new minister thinks everything is black and white. There are no shades of grey for him. I just switch off and think about my shopping list during the sermon now.' Later, at a dinner party, the lady sitting next to me, Mrs B, found out that I was a minister and almost immediately told me, 'I don't go to church any more. Both my parents died 15 years ago. At the same time, the Church of Scotland was letting into the ministry a man who had been in prison. It just wasn't right. The Church should stick to its moral principles about right and wrong. When everything else is changing the Church is the one thing which should never change.' I have to say that I personally found it easier to sympathize with Mrs A than Mrs B. It could be argued that, in terms of faith development, I was closer to Mrs A than I was to Mrs B. But then it is possible that Mrs A's new minister might have been a better pastor for Mrs B if he had been around at the time. I would have liked to try to help Mrs B, assuming, of course, first that she felt she had a problem, and second that she was asking for help, but I suspect that I would have found it just as difficult within the boundaries of a more private and defined pastoral setting as I did in fact find it sitting next to her at a dinner party.

Implicit in this discussion there is an issue of both theoretical and practical importance. Is conjunctive faith the most appropriate basis for pastoral care in a postmodern world? Or, is there the need for a diversity of different forms of pastoral care? Does progression from one stage of faith development to another necessarily imply movement towards a superior stage of faith development? Fowler has made it clear that his faith development theory relates to the *way* in which people believe and not to the *content* of the belief system. There are, however, those who believe that this distinction is not viable. Recently the British and Foreign Bible Society sponsored a conference at Cardiff University on 'The Bible and Pastoral Practice', at which Les Steele of Seattle Pacific University reflected upon Fowler's work in the light of Ephesians 4.11–16, arguing that 'mature faith has to do with what we believe and know to be true'.

The passage indicates that if we are to mature in faith then we will increase in our knowledge of the essential beliefs of our faith and come to a sense of stable doctrine . . . This knowledge is contrasted with the instability of someone who is 'tossed to and fro' by new and diverse beliefs that may blow in . . . Although there is little direct reference in these verses to the process of maturation, it seems that it points to learning the contents of the apostolic tradition, being willing to learn from pastors and teachers, and live out this faith with other members of the Christian community. We can only mature as we come to know and accept the truth of the apostolic tradition and then in turn learn and live this in community and service. (Steele 2000, 4)

It is not difficult to draw parallels between this understanding of mature faith and that which lies behind the 'applied theology' approach to pastoral care outlined in Chapter Two. It is essentially propositional in character. For Steele, the understanding of mature faith set out in Ephesians 4 is not compatible with Fowler's thesis.

With Fowler's definition of faith, you can be a stage 4 Christian today and tomorrow a stage 4 atheist and the level of maturity is unaffected. Whereas in Ephesians 4, the appropriation of orthodoxy is one of the norms of faith, in Fowler the way in which one holds faith is the norm. (Steele 2000, 8)

Two points may be made in response to Steele. The first is that it is possible for someone who might be identified as having a stage 6 conjunctive faith to hold deeply to some quite fundamental beliefs without necessarily having to impose these beliefs upon others. Fowler himself identifies as having stage 7 universalizing faith Thomas Merton and Mother Teresa. No one would consider either of these individuals as being other than deeply committed Catholics who could combine their own profound convictions with an openness to others. They did not have to try and convert them but rather were prepared to learn in a way which deepened their own faith. In the three case studies set out below, Frank, a minister who would not I think object to being described as a conservative evangelical, relates with an openness to others which does not compromise his own sense of theological identity.

The second point which can be made in response to Steele is to recognize (with him) that Fowler's stages are indeed inherently normative and progressive. Both Mrs A's minister and Mrs B would probably regard conjunctive faith as distinctly inferior to, a falling away from, the moral principles of orthodox, synthetic–conventional faith. Yet ministry in postmodern society requires the ability to empathize with and understand a wider range of people. This ought to be possible the further one progresses along the spectrum of faith development. It is more reasonable to expect a caring ministry towards those at a stage of faith through which one has passed – and hopefully understood. If so, then perhaps ministry to a wide range of people in a post-modern society requires some of the flexibility and openness which is characteristic of conjunctive faith.

What would such a ministry look like? We find some clues, I think, in following the three stories recounted by Frank, whose ministry is set in a large city-centre church. This is a gathered congregation with a long and distinguished history but now seeking new ways of engaging with the diverse community within which it is located. This community is one in which few people live but which is home to prominent international finan-cial institutions and the entertainment industry. Frank himself has reflected deeply upon postmodernism, and the following three cases are offered in response to a request to reflect upon the relationship between theory and practice in his ministry.

MINISTRY AND POSTMODERNITY: THREE CASE STUDIES

THE POSTMODERN TRAVELLER

Paula is from South Africa, working in Scotland with ambitions to live in the USA. At 26, she is a qualified graphic artist, with a passion for the creative arts. Her family back-ground is Baptist, but she has become ill at ease with that pattern of the Church and Christian expression. She has begun to explore Celtic spirituality.

It was this Celtic connection which first attracted her to our city-centre congregation: the call of the adventure of a church learning to be a 'church without walls' in the midst of business, entertainment and homeless sectors of the city.

The congregational ethos is very different from her tradi-tion, more liturgically sophisticated and musically formal. She is attracted to the 'lack of cliché' in the prayers and preaching.

What does pastoral care mean for this questioning enthusiast for life? She has decided to associate with the congregation, but was wary of the membership structure. She represents many who are spiritually alert but institutionally allergic.

The pastoral support lies in her occasional involvement with a small group which explores Celtic spirituality and other events on that theme. The occasions for meeting are not at home or in church, but for a cappuccino in a local coffee shop. Her area of service has been her skill in graphic design as we have worked together on a publicity project.

Paula is an avid film-goer and has joined with an association in Sheffield that explores film and theology. She is not interested in a formal group, but arranges ad hoc film visits with a chance to chat over a drink in the bar later. So far our discussions on current films have touched on the nature of community, the meaning of redemption, the nature of God, the need to play to be fully human. Bible passages and film scripts interweave in the conversation.

For the pastoral traveller, pastoral care is 'on the hoof', affirming her professional gifts in the cause of mission but not expecting her to support church structure, and entering into dialogue with her worldview through a medium she appreciates.

THE POSTMODERN SEEKER

Colin is a Buddhist – or was until a few months ago. At 52, he is a successful business consultant, has been divorced and has recently remarried a widow who happens to be an elder of our congregation.

Colin is a man of great intelligence, energy and warm humanity. He has travelled the world and faced some very risky situations. His spiritual search since university days has been the way of Zen Buddhism and martial arts.

Through his wife, he began attending church, and easily made friends. Congregational work among homeless people attracted his attention and drew him into practical service. Conversations about life and faith were lively and friendly.

His wife's friend became very ill and my colleague had prayed with them all over a period of time for her recovery. Sadly, that was not to be. The friend died. Colin had shared in the times of prayer and had spoken appreciatively of the help received.

Shortly afterwards, after a communion service, Colin approached me in a very agitated state. My assumption was that it had something to do with the death of the friend, but I was wrong. The communion service had affected him deeply. He spoke of being touched by something far bigger than himself., His tears were not tears of sadness, but of joy at the discovery of something he could not name. He had felt unable to receive the bread and wine but he had sensed a presence.

My colleague had preached on the Beatitudes that morning. Together we thought back through the aspects of spiritual need and search that were described there, the attitudes which open us to the blessings of God. Together we realized that Colin was experiencing the 'blessing of God', and prayed that God would open his eyes further.

In the following weeks he read the Gospel of John, received communion and became vividly aware of the love of God and the person of Jesus. We met weekly for an hour to talk through his questions. In time he joined a group that helped him on his journey.

He speaks freely of being found by God and of the significance of Jesus. He talks of new attitudes to people and his work. He intends to be confirmed.

His Buddhist background has given him a spiritual discipline and he often speaks of areas of convergence while affirming the Lordship of Christ as the one who fulfils his deepest searching.

Postmodern pastoring means being open to the searcher and being unembarrassed about addressing the spiritual discoveries that come to light. It is about sharing the journey together and letting Christ join us both.

THE POSTMODERN VICTIM

Derek (29) and Gillian (19) appear at the church door. They have arrived in the city from the islands, homeless, jobless and friendless. Money has run out and they are desperate for help. Approaches to the council have proved fruitless – not priority if there are no children or no physical or mental illness.

Where to start? Contact an agency and find directions.

Only night shelters available. One look at the girl, who is the same age as my daughter, and the decision is clear that they should not be allowed to face that situation if it can be avoided. Questions of being conned pass through the mind and are dismissed. It is my risk. Money is exchanged to pay for the B&B for the night and the address of another agency which might help.

Next day they are given good advice by the agency and the possibility of a house in a couple of days. The contact person agrees they are genuine. We agree to offer financial support until the system can come into play for them.

Postmodernity is marked by the breakdown of community and its victims float by the church door at any time. Pastoring may involve being the only committed person on the horizon when the system seems to fail or be unable to respond quickly enough. It means knowing enough of the system to be able to respond to the crisis and, where possible, to have established a good rapport with people in various community agencies. Pastoring is based upon partnerships of knowledge and skill. At times, it means taking the risk of being let down rather taking the risk of becoming cynical.

I wish to reflect upon these cases from two perspectives. First I will consider them in terms of Frank's account of them. Perhaps I should repeat here the information that these cases were offered to me by Frank as a result of a conversation in which I asked him if he could provide me with some case material which reflected the themes of postmodernity. These three cases therefore are quite intentional attempts to describe pastoral ministry in a postmodern context. It is legitimate to explore how far this attempt succeeds. But second, another level of analysis is possible and that is to enquire how far ministry is an adequate response to the postmodern context. In particular I wish to explore how far Frank's ministry is congruent with Fowler's delineation of the characteristics of conjunctive faith.

First, then, how far do these cases reflect the condition of postmodernity? In a sense Paula is the epitome of postmodern woman. She is a traveller, a citizen of the world. With roots in South Africa, she is (for the time being) in Britain, hopefully on the way to the USA. Yet although she is in a sense passing through, while she is here she is very much present to and in relationship with her environment. One senses a joyful embracing of the reality of her present moment. And if she is a traveller in a literal, geographical sense she is also on the move in a metaphorical, spiritual sense. Reacting against her Baptist background she has found a temporary home in a Presbyterian church with a strong liturgical tradition. And for the time being it *is* 'home' for her in the sense that she makes it home – though not to the extent of taking out a mortgage with the long-term commitment which that might imply. We also see in Paula the postmodern quest for a relevant spirituality and her attempt to find this within the Celtic tradition. While she does not wish to become a member of the congregation, she is willing to contribute her skills as a graphic artist. In her professional life and in her leisure activities, Paula is every inch a postmodern woman. Her qualification as a graphic artist and her passion for film reflect the postmodern concern for image and for the power of image to point beyond itself, raising questions of fundamental importance.

Colin, too, bears many of the marks of postmodern man. Like Paula, he has been a traveller in both the literal and the metaphorical senses. He is a business consultant, offering his expertise on an ad hoc basis whenever it is wanted, committed to each task for the period of his involvement, and then moving on. His spiritual journey has taken him into Zen Buddhism, but this does not prevent him from sharing in the religious practices of his new Presbyterian wife. He joins in intercessory prayer for a sick friend and attends a communion service (but does not at that point receive the elements of bread and wine). We are told of the profound effect which the communion service had on Colin and of his subsequent conversion to the Christian faith. Yet this conversion did not entail a total rejection of what had been important to him in his Buddhist faith. Rather, he continues to value the spiritual discipline of that faith and to continue to explore areas of convergence, embracing the complexity and paradox of his new situation rather than seeing issues in terms of the truth and falsehood of each religious tradition.

Derek and Gillian are also part of postmodern society, yet their story is very different from those of Paula and Colin. Significantly, Frank describes them as postmodern 'victims'. Paula is described as 'traveller' and Colin as 'searcher', both active in the pursuit of their own destiny, certainly constrained by the boundaries set by their own choices, but within those boundaries having and exercising a degree of freedom of choice. One senses that Derek and Gillian have had very little choice in their own destiny, other than to flee from a situation which was intolerable. People do not become homeless by choice. Behind every homeless person there is a human tragedy. One can only begin to speculate upon the circumstances of this young couple 'from the islands' and what caused them to leave home and head for the city. They are rightly described as 'postmodern victims', the products of the fragmentation of family life and of the breakdown of community.

Such then are the cases described by Frank as examples of pastoral care in a postmodern context. So far we have explored the features of postmodernity in the context. But what of the pastoral care offered in that context? My thesis is that in Fowler's understanding of conjunctive faith we catch a glimpse of the kind of faith which is required for ministry in the context of postmodernity. Conjunctive faith has already been described (p. 110) in terms of the need experienced by some adults in mid-life to move beyond the previous stage of individuative–reflective faith (which, it will be recalled, Fowler related to the consciousness of modernity) because they found this kind of faith inadequate to cope with their experience of reality. In conjunctive faith, truth is seen to be more complex, issues less clearly defined and a need is perceived to hold apparently contradictory views simultaneously, each of them necessary to encompass the truth of things. Truths adequate for the grounding of life come to be seen as multidimensional and as containing paradoxes. There is a new 'epistemological humility' and a more porous and receptive stance towards the reality of others.

What can we say about the pastoral ministry of Frank in this situation? More, surely, than what he would claim for himself, and two things in particular. We observe, first, many of the characteristics of conjunctive faith on the part of Frank and, second, his own grounding in the Christian narrative. In Frank's ministry with Paula we observe his deep respect for her as a person, his acceptance of the fact that she wished to be associated with the congregation without taking on the full commitment of membership (in fact her commitment was probably greater than many who are 'paper' members); we observe his encouragement to her to pursue her own spiritual journey; we observe too his understanding of ministry 'on the hoof', of pastoral relationships very different from (but probably more effective than) the 50-minute hour of the counsellor; and we observe his willingness to meet her on her own ground, whether in the coffee shop or bar; above all, we observe his deep respect for her as a person in her own right and not as a potential church member. We observe this same deep respect for the person in Frank's ministry with Colin. We do not catch any flavour of Frank seeking to undermine Colin's Buddhist faith, but rather an acceptance of him both as the husband of one of the elders of the church and as a person in his own right. Even after Colin converts to the Christian faith there is no attempt to persuade him of the error of his previous beliefs, but rather an encouragement to draw upon what was good in that system and to seek integration in some higher truth which would inevitably contain a degree of unresolved paradox.

Yet in both of these pastoral relationships Frank did not pretend to be other than he was, a minister of the gospel. A deep acceptance of the other involves neither the veiling of one's identity nor the loss of integrity. In the post-film conversations with Paula, the discussion was profoundly theological, the Christian narrative in dialogue with other narratives but, out of its own power and integrity, making its contribution to emerging truth. With Colin, the critical incident was the communion service in which the heart of the gospel is set forth in word and symbol. Here was manifested a pastoral care which was open both to the particularity of one spiritual journey and to the ability of Word and sacrament to bring healing and peace.

It is at this point that James Fowler's understanding of 'stages of faith' provides some insights into the kind of ministry which is required in contemporary society. It will be recalled that Fowler's initial studies were directed towards identifying seven stages of faith development which had a degree of commonality shared by most of the population. While these were age-related, particularly in the early stages, this was not a precise correlation, and indeed Fowler indicated that in adulthood people might 'plateau' at a certain stage, not progressing beyond stage 4 (synthetic–conventional faith) or stage 5 (individuative–reflective faith). It will also be remembered that Fowler postulated a correlation between three of the seven stages of faith (stages 4, 5 and 6) with three phases of cultural consciousness (the premodern, the modern and the postmodern) which in turn he correlated with three tempers, three ways of being in the world (the orthodox, the progressive and the postmodern). Simply to identify the variables indicates the complexity of the task of ministry in contemporary society. First, people generally, and not just members of churches, are at different stages of faith development which will manifest itself in their way of being (or not being) 'religious'. Second, ministers, whatever their denominational label, may find themselves most comfortable with one particular stage of faith and indeed, ministers exhibiting most of Fowler's stages of faith are found right across the spectrum of denominational allegiance. Further, if we take seriously Fowler's work on cultural consciousness, society as a whole will reflect in its cultural values all three phases of cultural consciousness. Last, but certainly not least, congregations may exhibit characteristics which correspond to each of these three modes of being in the world. There are certainly orthodox congregations, and there are congregations which are relatively more progressive. Whether there are any congregations which could be described as 'postmodern' is doubtful.

MODELS OF MINISTRY

Since this book is predominantly about the ordained ministry, I now wish to extend this argument further by attempting to describe how ministers at different stages of faith may function in contemporary society. Let it be said right away that in this analysis there is no implication of moral judgement. It is not implied that a minister at 'Fowler stage 5' is better than one at 'Fowler stage 4' and that a 'stage 6 (or 7)' minister is somehow superior to both of them. It is maintained, however, that they will function differently in their ministries, that they will bring different gifts and attitudes to ministry, and will find themselves comfortable in different settings of ministry. Building upon Fowler's work it is possible to sketch out three different models of ministry. Let us then examine how Fowler's three tempers might be reflected in different models of ministerial practice.

THE MINISTER OF ORTHODOX TEMPER

If we assume that ministers of orthodox temper share the same characteristics as are generally held by people of synthetic–conventional faith, then we might expect them to find their authority outside of themselves, either in the Bible or in the tradition of the Church. They will tend to take a literal view of the Scriptures or of the teachings of the Church. They will have very clear ideas of right and wrong, particularly in the sphere of sexual ethics. Mission will be understood as going out in order to convert unbelievers to the one true faith. For them outreach equals 'in-grab'. Ministers of orthodox temper are often very good at building up happy congregations of people of similar temper. It is no accident that amid the decline of mainstream Christianity, the centres of growth are, more often than not, those congregations which are conservative both in theology and in moral values. In such congregations, people find their own values affirmed and a sense of security when all around them is in a state of rapid change. While Fowler talks of an orthodox temper, it might be more correct to describe it as a conservative one. It should not, however, be thought that the orthodox temper is confined to conservative-evangelical churches. It is not unknown for allegedly radical political groups to have their fundamentalists for whom 'Clause 4' (of the Labour Party Constitution) or the writings of Karl Marx take on the character of Holy Writ. Neither are the secular psychotherapies free from their orthodox believers. It is not unknown for the collected works of Freud to be regarded as the Supreme Rule of faith and life.

When a minister of orthodox temper is inducted to a new congregation, there are likely to be varying reactions among its members. When there is a radical change of theological emphasis, those who have been primarily responsible for calling the new minister will generally be pleased with their choice. At last the True Gospel is being preached. The true believers will bring friends looking for an authoritative word and the congregation will begin to grow. The new man (and it usually is a man) lets people know where he stands. There will be clear rules about whom he will and will not marry – a man and a woman living at the same address need not apply. True, not all members of the congregation will be equally happy. The middle-aged couple who supported their new, young, enthusiastic minister until their daughter went to live with her boyfriend realize that the issue is not as black and white as the minister makes out – at least, not in the case of their daughter. The woman of progressive temper (like the one I described in a previous chapter) will switch off during the sermon and think about her shopping list – until she finds another congregation or stops going to church altogether.

Ministers of orthodox temper are usually sincere, dedicated ministers who work hard at their preaching, which is almost certainly Bible-based and expository, inculcating in those members of their congregations knowledge of and love for the Scriptures. Theologically, their emphasis will be upon the atonement, upon the saving work of Christ and upon the need for repentance and faith. They will be pastorally committed to the needy both inside and outside the congregation, though ministry to those outside may be judged by its success in bringing in the outsiders to share the beliefs of the insiders.

The above description of the minister of orthodox temper is of course a caricature, but not, I hope, to the extent that it totally distorts the truth. It must be recognized that there is in this understanding of ministry great strength and that it has always been central to the growth and maintenance of the Church. Neither is it insignificant (as I suggested in an earlier chapter) that much of the important engagement with postmodern ideas has come from the conservative-evangelical wing of the Church. It is significant, too, that evangelicals more than any other group have grasped the significance of the communications revolution which is central to postmodern society. This should perhaps surprise us. With the Scriptures being so central to the conservative-evangelical position, the defence of their integrity and the communication of their message must inevitably have high priority.

THE MINISTER OF PROGRESSIVE TEMPER

If again we assume that ministers of progressive temper have much in common with those who demonstrate the general characteristics of individuative-reflective faith, we can begin to discern something of the nature of their ministry. Such ministers are the heirs of the Enlightenment. Owing no allegiance to any external authority, they will accord to both Scripture and tradition the respect which they personally believe they deserve. Rejecting literalist interpretations of Scripture, they will nevertheless believe that the teaching of the Bible is normative for Christian living. They will bring to its interpretations all the tools of modern scholarship. At theological college, they took Bultmann's demythologizing project in their stride, wondering what all the fuss had been about. Creeds and confessions they regard as important historical documents, guidelines rather than straitjackets. If truth were told they have a somewhat ambivalent attitude to the Church, a love-hate relationship born out of the intercourse of frustration and possibility. Their vision for the Church is ecumenical but they have adjusted to the possibility that progress is slow – and that in some local situations it may be too late to make any difference. In their pastoral work, they will be as open towards the parish and community as to the local congregation. The occasional offices, baptisms, weddings and funerals, will be regarded as opportunities for mission in the widest sense, which they will probably understand as serving people in the name of Christ. Theologically, their emphasis will be upon creation and incarnation, upon a God who loved the world before he loved the Church, and Christ who took the initiative in making himself available to women and men in their time of need. In their pastoral work, they will not be afraid to take on board the insights of the social sciences. They will listen more than they will talk and will not rush to quick judgements. In their preaching they will be more concerned to emphasize social justice than personal morality. They may find stimulation and satisfaction in different kinds of chaplaincy work, in ministry in the secular arena, believing that sometimes this is of more relevance than propping up the local congregation. Indeed, some of their frustration with the local congregation may lead them into a variety of extra-congregational activities, not only chaplaincies but demanding convenerships in community and church organizations at regional and national level, especially if they have 'a safe pair of hands'.

If truth were told, ministers of orthodox and progressive tempers find it hard to understand one another and this is a source of continuing tension within the churches. Progressives regard the orthodox as obscurantist and irrelevant, out of touch with real life, holding on to a theological position which is in itself a barrier to the communication of the gospel, which (claim the progressives) is about grace rather than judgement. Conversely, the orthodox believe that progressives have exchanged their inheritance of truth for a mess of modern pottage, supposedly relevant but not in the end sustaining either the Church or individuals. In any case (claim the orthodox) it is the conservative churches which are growing. The breakdown in communication is serious and damaging. This has been noted by Fowler and a possible reason for it identified:

> The particular virulence of the struggles between these two tempers may be partially understood by recognizing that both these ways of seeing and being in the world are presently under threat. Though this sense of threat may be only partially conscious in both camps, it seems growingly clear that we are in a time of pervasive transition in the structures of cultural and social consciousness. The shrillness of the representatives of both the orthodox and progressive alignments may result from their sense of the loss of familiar certainties in the face

of a revolution in consciousness so powerful that it is likely to dwarf the impact of the eighteenth-century Enlightenment. (Fowler 1996, 172)

Fowler goes on to set out what he believes are the characteristics of the postmodern experience, an experience which, as we noted earlier, is a real one whether or not people have heard of 'postmodernism', let alone understood the philosophical theories which accompany it. Pursuing the argument outlined above, we must now ask whether there is an approach to ministry which relates to the postmodern temper.

MINISTRY FOR POSTMODERN TIMES

For the sake of symmetry, I might have chosen to speak of 'the minister of postmodern temper', but I have not done so. My assumption in speaking of ministers of orthodox and progressive tempers was that they (more or less) shared the social and cultural values of the groups to which they belong and that their ministry was worked out in terms of these values. Is it possible for a person to take on board the social and cultural values of postmodernity and still remain within the ordained ministry of the Church? There is evidence that there are limits to the diversity of belief and conduct which the Church can tolerate, particularly if that diversity emerges into the public domain. Anthony Freeman in his book *God In Us: A Case for Christian Humanism* rejected what he considered to be traditional understandings of the nature of God and found himself relieved of his duties as a priest of the Church of England. Significantly he saw his position as one which attempted to move beyond the current tension between conservative and liberal theologies. One of the most interesting attempts to engage with young people in terms of postmodern culture was the Nine O'Clock Service in Sheffield. Making full use of contemporary modes of communication, it was pioneering new ways of presenting the gospel which would have lessons for the whole Church. It has not fulfilled its potential, at least partly because of publicity consequent upon the failure of one of the leaders to observe appropriate sexual boundaries. Those who live by the media die by the media! It is clear that ordination vows are not compatible with either total diversity of theological opinion or complete ethical relativism. Instead, therefore, of speaking of the minister of postmodern temper we must ask what kind of ministry is needed for postmodern times.

My argument is that in order to minister effectively in post-modern times, it is necessary to take a somewhat more selective attitude towards its values. While having an understanding of the social and cultural forces shaping contemporary postmodern society and the lives of people in it, a ministry of postmodern times will take a much more 'pick and mix' approach to the values of postmodernity – which, I suppose, in itself is a very postmodern attitude! There is much that is of value in the post-modern temper. It is arguable that a weakness of ministry rooted in both the orthodox and progressive tempers is that the practitioners became locked into the social and cultural consciousness of which they were part, with a consequent inability to see beyond their own basic assumptions. The postmodern emphasis upon the importance of perspective provides the basis for a certain detachment towards values held in both Church and society, and a freedom to respond in an appropriate manner which does not compromise the integrity of ministry.

In a strange way, this postmodern religious context provides a fresh context in which the Christian narrative may enter into constructive encounter with contemporary society. The days of Christendom are over; the Christian narrative no longer has unquestioned acceptance as the supreme rule of faith and life. To that extent the postmodern critique of metanarrative has been effective. Yet, paradoxically, in a pluralistic age, when many different narratives are striving to be heard, the biblical narrative can no longer be marginalized. It takes its place amid the Babel of all the other narratives which impinge upon the conscious (and the unconscious) minds of men and women. The extent to which the Christian narrative makes a contribution to human well-being will depend upon the extent to which it rings true in the hearts and minds of postmodern people.

To be a pastor in postmodern times requires a deep under-standing of the pressures, cultural, societal and religious, which impinge upon the lives of those who live in contemporary society. Yet such understanding does not imply an uncritical acceptance of its values and philosophy. Pastoral care within this society also requires an ability to live and minister out of a conviction of the relevance of the biblical narrative in all its fullness. This does not lead to any compulsion to impose biblical truth upon others, but stems from a conviction upon the truth and integrity of the narrative itself. Those engaged in pastoral care will also enjoy the freedom to minister out of the integrity of their own narrative. Gerkin, as we saw earlier, spoke of pastoral care standing in the gap between the story of the individual and the larger Christian story; the Christian pastor stands in the gap, as the bearer both of his own story and of the larger Christian story. To be sensitive to the ways in which that larger story can help to interpret the life story of the other while fully respecting the integrity of the other is to exercise a ministry of pastoral care which has its own integrity. To function in this way requires a deep awareness of self and others, and a capacity for reflection upon the part of those engaged in the practice of ministry as exemplified in the ministry of Frank in the three cases set out earlier in this chapter. To minister in postmodern times one must be a 'reflective practitioner', to use a phrase and introduce a concept which in recent discussions has thrown light on the relationship between theory and practice in a number of different professions.

In the final two chapters I shall set out five examples of pastoral care as described by the ministers involved themselves. On the basis of reflection upon these cases I shall argue that the concept of reflective practice leads us to a deeper understanding of the nature of pastoral integrity in a postmodern world.

CHAPTER SEVEN

Pastoral Ministry Today

What are the realities of pastoral ministry in today's world? At the planning stage of this book, I realized two things. The first was that it was over ten years since I had been involved in pastoral ministry on a full-time basis. The second was that if my thesis is correct, namely that there is much high-quality pastoral care being practised in congregations and communities, then some of that should be accessible. I therefore wrote to about 20 colleagues in ministry and asked if they would be willing to share with me accounts of some aspects of their ministry. This was not a random sample. Some of the people I approached were people whom I knew to be deeply reflective about their ministry; some were former students in the MTh course who were used to a case study approach. In the event about 15 people sent me over 30 cases illustrating different aspects of ministry. All were ordained ministers from at least three different denominations; most were engaged in ministry on a full-time basis, though some were part-time or non-stipendiary; most but not all of them were working in parishes, and a third of them were women. In the event I have drawn upon 15 cases submitted by ten ministers, with five of these cases set out below.

In this chapter, I will try to set out what I believe to be the main characteristics of pastoral care. In order to do so, I will allow several ministers to speak for themselves as they describe pastoral situations in which they have been deeply involved. All of the cases will be set out first, more or less as they have been written up by the ministers. I have chosen this approach because I believe that a straight reading through of the material points to the depth and richness of much contemporary pastoral ministry. In each case I will highlight some points of particular interest, exploring some of the issues raised in terms of contemporary writing in pastoral studies. The names of all the ministers have been changed.

PASTORAL CARE AND THE POSTMODERN FAMILY

Anne is minister of a suburban congregation. In this case study she describes her ministry in a complicated family situation which reveals ever-increasing layers of complexity within the family relationships.

> I had a request to baptize the baby of a young couple in the parish. When I married them I invited them to a church membership class, so neither of them were members of the church but they said they would come to the next class. The wife's sister then phoned me to ask if I would baptize her second baby. She is a single mother, the father of her second baby being different from the father of her first. She lives with her mother who is divorced from her husband. With this background Alan (a student on placement) and I set out on the visit. When we got into the visit, a number of other things emerged: (a) when Helen (the married sister) gave birth she got an infection, the result of which is that she is very unlikely to have any more children. Clearly she and her husband are very distressed. They feel the infection occurred because of negligence on the part of hospital staff and they are taking advice on suing the Health Board. As well as the distress and the devastation at not being able to have more children, Helen continues to suffer physically; (b) the grandmother of the two mothers was present. Her husband had died recently and she was trying to cope with her grief in the midst of other family problems which were overshadowing hers; (c) her son, aged 47 and the father of the two young mothers, was a patient in a local hospice. It had been hoped that he would be able to attend the baptismal service but they knew that his death was imminent. Although he was divorced from his wife, they had remained on good terms. His new partner was around, and the position of both women in the event had to be balanced. In fact he died the day before the baptism and the funeral took place on the following Saturday.

I have called this case 'Pastoral Care and the Postmodern Family' because the family situation described reflects the complexities of much contemporary life, notably of marriage bonds dissolving and re-forming, of marriages ending but with relationships continuing. We see too a hint of postmodern consumerism in the suggestion that the Health Board could be sued for negligence. If something goes wrong then it is someone's fault and that someone must be made to pay. As it happened, Anne herself had a legal background and was careful not to give an opinion on the issue of possible hospital negligence. (Interestingly, the student on placement was a mature student with wide experience in social work whose previous background might have inclined him to take a different view of 'advocacy'.)

In subsequent conversations with Anne, the following points emerged as she described that first and subsequent visits to the family. First, she was aware that there were many people involved in the situation with very different needs. If this was a pastoral situation of great complexity, most ministers will testify that it was not uniquely so. Second, she claimed that what a minister actually said in that acute situation was not all that significant. It was 'being there' that was important, words would come later. She did speak, however, of the difficulty of the pre-funeral visit, trying, amid the chaos of visitors coming and going, to find out something of the life of the man who had died. She was aware of conducting a baptism for a family the day after a major bereavement – and then of conducting a funeral service a few days after the baptism.

MINISTRY AND COMPLEXITY

Anne's story illustrates the complexity of the family situations in which pastoral ministry must be exercised. When a minister visits a bereaved family one simply accepts that one is unlikely to have a quiet private conversation with whoever is most deeply affected by the death. That will come later. The visit of Anne to a home simply, on the face of it, to discuss a baptism illustrates the complexity of the family relationships in which a minister may become involved. She went to make arrangements for the baptism of Helen's baby, ostensibly a happy event, but found herself ministering to a family in the midst of multiple problems. Helen herself had caught an infection and was distressed at the thought of having no more children; her sister was a single mother with two children by different fathers; her grandmother was grieving the recent death of her own husband; Helen's father was about to die; her parents were divorced and there was her dying father's new partner to be considered. Any one of these situations could have led to a pastoral relationship of some depth. In the event ministry was exercised through two acts of worship, closely related in time, a baptism and a funeral, as well as through visits to different members of the family during and after this period. It was during the subsequent visits, after the many relatives had departed, that Anne was able to sit and listen to the separate stories of each of the central characters in this drama. More will be said in due course of the pastoral importance of the way in which the baptismal service and the funeral were conducted.

ON FINDING WORDS

Despite Anne's claim that what a minister says in acute situations is of far less importance than their capacity for 'being there', words are very much part of the stock-in-trade of ministry. We cannot ignore the fact that ordination is quite explicitly to Word and sacrament. In this regard at least, pastors stand in stark contrast to counsellors. Counsellors tend to be people of few words. When words are spoken these are chosen for their content and measured for their mood to be an accurate empathic response to the thoughts, feelings and needs expressed by their clients. In the counselling relationship they tend to reveal very little about themselves.

Psychodynamically oriented counsellors may observe a 'rule of abstinence' in relation to the clients, believing that this is essential to the therapeutic process. Counsellors are unlikely to have any contact with clients beyond the limits of that single professional relationship, and indeed would regard such contact as something to be avoided. In contrast, pastoral relationships between carer and cared for are generally very different from that between counsellor and client, normally being part of a network of wider relationships. In the setting of a local congregation, ministers are encountered in a variety of roles. They preach sermons, celebrate sacraments, argue in committees and socialize at parties. Their spouses, children and sometimes their parents are known to the congregation. This means that in their pastoral relationships ministers can seldom be anonymous. Perhaps more fundamentally, ministers have a different relationship to words. Ordained to a ministry of Word and sacrament, they are expected to be able to use words creatively and wisely; in public prayer, certainly within those traditions with extempore forms of prayer, they are valued for their ability to keep on finding new words every Sunday to express the age-old hopes, fears, failings and longings of a diverse group of people. Much pastoral care is a search for the right words. This is because pastoral care is exercised not simply through the one-to-one relationship, as in counselling, but through the whole myriad of activities which constitute ministry.

For Anne, her ministry extended far beyond the pre-baptismal visit, to the baptismal service itself (which was anticipated), to a number of home visits surrounding the death of the baby's grandfather and a funeral (which were not). She described her frustration at an unsatisfactory pre-funeral visit. People were coming and going, and besides offering what comfort she could to the bereaved family, she was trying to find the right words for the funeral service. This is an important part of pastoral ministry which is often not appreciated. It is possible to attend funeral services and to leave not knowing whose funeral it was! A funeral service which is good from a pastoral theological perspective is one which tells the story and celebrates the life of the one who has died. When the deceased is well known to the minister that task is comparatively easy, though there are still facts, impressions, things to be said (or not said) to be checked out with the family. When, as is more common, the person who has died is less well known or even unknown to the minister, the task is more difficult. The words – or the raw material for the words – have to be provided by those who knew the deceased. The aim must always be to be real, to help the family and friends give thanks and begin to let go of this person, neither causing embarrassment by painting the picture of a saint who never was nor causing pain by saying things better left unsaid. To obtain the information needed to achieve this is a rare pastoral skill. Many words may be used in a formal tribute, painting a detailed picture of the person who has died; sometimes a few deft phrases in a prayer of thanksgiving, crafted as skilfully as a Rolf Harris cartoon, convey the essence of the person.

One more aspect of Anne's ministry in this situation is worthy of attention. This was not any baptism she was conducting. It was a baptism where the grandfather had died the previous day. Neither was it any funeral service. It was a funeral service where many members of the family had joined together in comparatively happier circumstances a few days earlier. Anne did not in fact conduct these two services as though they took place in isolation from one another. At the baptism she mentioned the death of the grandfather and how much he had been looking forward to being present. At the funeral she mentioned the baptism, using words in a way which addressed the reality of that family, hopefully helping them to move on as, in the words of both the baptismal service and the funeral service, she helped the family to see its story in the light of the Christian story and its promises of new beginnings and new life, of forgiveness for what is past and hope for the future.

WHEN A BABY IS BORN DEAD

Barry, a parish minister and part-time hospital chaplain, describes his pastoral care of a couple whose baby is stillborn.

The labour ward sister telephoned to advise me that a mother was about to deliver a stillborn child and to ask if I was available to attend if requested. The sister telephoned some 30 minutes later to say that the child, a boy, had been delivered and that the parents, Brian and Kathleen, would be glad to see me. It was agreed that I should visit the hospital in about an hour's time as the mother was wanting to have a bath, but on arriving at the hospital I found that the mother had already been discharged and that the couple had gone home.

The sister told me the couple were married, in their late thirties, and that they already had one two-year-old daughter. The parents had known for some 48 hours that their baby would be stillborn and they had been told of the opportunity to see the chaplain and to arrange for a funeral service for their baby at the Rose Garden of a cemetery in the city. The sister reported that, as well as being distressed, the couple seemed very anxious as to what they wanted to do. I also learned that one of the grandfathers (as it turned out Brian's father) was a minister. As it was now late in the evening (11.45 p.m. – why do these events always happen at night!) I agreed with Sister that I would telephone them in the morning.

When I called the following morning I spoke to Kathleen, who was full of apologies for my 'wasted' visit to the hospital and explained that she had wanted to be out of the hospital and home as quickly as possible. Having assured her that my visit had been anything but wasted, we agreed that I should visit them at home later in the day.

Within moments of my arriving at their home, Brian launched into a long and rambling questioning about whether their baby had been a real baby or, because it was stillborn, had never been more than a foetus. Although the stages of physical development could be traced, he wanted to know at what time a baby developed a soul, for he understood that it was a person's soul that goes to heaven. And with his father being a minister, and so to that extent being familiar with funeral arrangements, Brian was surprised that he had never heard about the Rose Garden and seemed suspicious about it.

In contrast to Brian's at times quite emotional conversation, Kathleen was much more self-contained. Although she understood Brian's concerns, she did not share them. Her baby had been alive, she had felt it kick and move and needed no further convincing that it was much more than 'just' a foetus. For her part Kathleen wondered if she had been able to say her 'goodbyes' in the hospital and was not sure if she needed to do anything more. She was also anxious that any kind of funeral service would involve a large number of people being present, as she felt quite sure she could not cope with that.

The practical questions of how long the Rose Garden had existed and what happened at the service and the fact that there need be no more people present than the pair of them were quickly and satisfactorily answered. The deeper question about the beginning of life and the need to say goodbye formed the greater part of the conversation.

In the course of the discussion I sought not to provide answers but to encourage Brian and Kathleen to explore the depth of their questions. I did, however, raise the issue of Brian's father, not only to help Brian and Kathleen see how their baby's death would affect the wider family but, given the fact that he was a minister, to ask if they saw a role for him in conducting the service. It was interesting to observe that following the initial statements in which each declared their position to me, I became increasingly incidental to the conversation as they entered into dialogue with one another.

Brian wondered if there was an answer to his question and what it would mean to him to conclude that there was not. Kathleen disliked the thought of the hospital disposing of her baby and began to wonder if a service would help her, not to say goodbye, but to affirm that this child would always be part of her family. The meeting ended after about 90 minutes on the understanding that when they had taken time to think things through, Brian and Kathleen would contact me with their decision. Kathleen called two days later to say they would like me to conduct a funeral service and that the pair of them would be the only people present.

INITIATIVE AND AVAILABILITY

A distinctive feature of pastoral care is that it is proactive. Counsellors (quite properly) do not go looking for clients. They, or the agencies for which they work, may advertise their services but essentially they wait for the initiative to be taken by prospective clients. There may then be a period of negotiation when counsellor and client will discuss whether the service offered by the counsellor is likely to meet the needs of the client. Then counselling proper begins.

Pastoral ministry is different. Within a congregation which has called a minister there is the expectation that he or she will visit. Sometimes these expectations are quite unrealistic, in terms of the regular visitation of all members of the congregation whether or not there is an expressed need. But there is also an appropriate expectation that where there is trouble the minister will call. If there is a bereavement within the congregation, the minister does not usually wait to be invited to visit, as we saw in the above case study. She calls, and it would usually be regarded as dereliction of duty if she did not. In the context of the parish, as opposed to the congregation, the situation is more ambiguous. Certainly as a parish minister in the late 1960s with a clearly defined geographical area which was 'my parish', it would not have been thought inappropriate and indeed was usually welcomed if I visited a home in the parish where there was trouble. That said, a visit to a home where someone was very ill had to be handled with great care lest the minister was seen as the harbinger of death. I suspect that while this proactive role of the minister may still be possible in country parishes and small towns, it may not be possible to the same extent in large urban areas.

It is arguable that a proactive pastoral ministry is only possible today on the basis of a ministry of availability. By this I mean that a pastoral ministry in the community can only be built upon a willingness to become involved in the life of a community, so that ministers become known not for the positions they hold but because of the people they are. Pastoral ministry can only be built upon personal integrity.

Hospital and hospice chaplains must also be proactive in their ministry of pastoral care. Chaplains who sit in their offices and wait for the telephone to ring are likely to drink many lonely cups of coffee. There is again an expectation on the part of those who appoint chaplains, whether churches or trusts, that chaplains will be deeply involved with patients, their families and staff. There will be thought nothing untoward in the chaplain visiting every patient in a ward and introducing him or herself. Just occasionally, a charge nurse who has had a bad experience of a visiting minister will express reservations about this practice, but where relationships of trust have been established between chaplain and ward staff, chaplains' visits are welcomed and used profitably. A general visit to everyone on the ward can create the opportunity for the sister to bring to the chaplain's notice any patient who is causing special concern. Yet this kind of general visiting requires certain techniques and (perhaps even more important) attitudes which leave patients in control of the relationship. Proactive hospital visiting must express availability without imposition. The hospital ward is a place neither for rabid evangelicals seeking to save souls nor for trainee counsellors looking for people on whom to hone their skills. Proactive hospital visiting is essentially an approach by one human being to another, the one making the approach having no preconceived ideas about what ought to happen. There must be sensitivity to the implicit contract which begins to be offered (or not, as the case may be) from the moment the patient begins to respond to the chaplain's approach.

Barry's ministry in this situation where a couple's baby has been stillborn is a good example of a ministry of initiative and availability. The hospital staff would have been unlikely to call Barry into this sensitive situation unless they knew him and, on the basis of that knowledge, were confident that he would be pastorally helpful. Such a reputation is hard won and easily lost. It is built upon a developing experience of the chaplain being available as a non-intrusive presence. Often apparently casual in its expression, it is built upon a chaplain's ability to take an appropriate initiative. All this is implicit in Barry's description of this piece of ministry, his going when asked, his uncomplaining going away when he was not needed, his going again to meet the couple at home, his availability to do what they wished, his giving them space and, above all, his non-imposition of answers.

ON NOT FINDING WORDS

In discussing the previous case, I highlighted the minister's need to find words. Here I address the other side of that coin, the need to be personally available without imposing one's own interpretation upon the situation. Sometimes, as we have seen when we analysed an ordinand's first foray into hospital visiting, there is a grace in having nothing to say. This is another such situation. 'In the course of the discussion I sought not to provide answers but to enable Brian and Kathleen to explore the depth of their questions.' Barry realized that at that point in time, no words of his would help. Yet from the depths of a pastoral relationship which manifests availability without imposition there often emerges a Word which transcends words. There is a sense in which the pastoral relationship is both parabolic, pointing beyond itself to a deeper grace, and poetic, evoking within the imagination images of transcendence.

A PRESBYTERIAN RESPONSE TO THE REQUEST FOR 'LAST RITES'

In this case Chris, a hospice chaplain, describes an aspect of ministry which is very common in hospital chaplaincy, namely a pastoral encounter in which depth is out of all proportion to length.

> At one o'clock in the morning, in my capacity as hospice chaplain I was phoned by the sister in charge of the Centre saying that the family of one of our patients was asking me to come in and perform the last rites for their dying father. I had spent time with the patient over the previous few days, and had made intermittent contact with the son and daughter of the family. I knew them to be vulnerable people in much need of support, and so, with the other staff, had given comfort and reassurance, appropriate to their needs. I knew them to be non-religious people with a 'nothing' approach to belief rather than being consciously atheistic – in other words they had never given religion much thought. I also knew them to be Protestant by background and

actively non-Catholic! I was puzzled, therefore, by the family's request for 'the last rites', an exclusively Roman Catholic sacrament, from someone they knew to be a non-denominational chaplain.

I expressed my puzzlement to the nursing sister. She was well aware of the circumstances, too, but she made it clear that the family were insisting, that she could not deflect them, and that they were becoming more and more distressed. So a short time later I found myself at the bedside of a dying elderly man, in the company of a distraught son and daughter. The patient was beyond my intervention, peaceful but close to death. The son and daughter were, however, much in need of support. The son almost threw himself on me when I arrived. 'Thank God you are here, minister' – he never could remember my name! 'You are just in time. We want the last rites for ma faither.' Gently but firmly I explained that the last rites was a Catholic issue and I knew they weren't Catholics. 'I ken that,' came the reply, 'but that's no' the point, son. Ma faither needs the last rites 'fore he dies. Or else he'll no' be a' right when he's deid.'

This was clearly not the moment to explain the meaning of the sacraments in the Roman Catholic tradition, nor a theology of the after-life, nor even the grace of God. This was a moment for responding to the needs of a family. And what were their needs? To 'do it right' for a dying man, to have covered all the bases, to let him pass from life having done their best for him right to the end.

So without further ado, I invited the son and daughter to sit down by the bedside. I pulled the screens around and sat on the edge of the bed. I read the 23rd Psalm and said a prayer, extempore, in good Presbyterian tradition! I cannot now remember the content of the prayer, but it was short and simple, and about believing the old man's life was in the hands of God, praying that he should go in peace, and asking God's blessing on those who would grieve for his passing. We sat in silence for a while, then I took my leave. I left the family to their vigil with their father. The old man died in the early hours of the morning. I have never seen the family again. The nursing staff told me the following day that they had coped better with the death than anyone expected.

There is, however, a short sequel to this story. Some

months later I was shopping in the local Safeway and I bumped into an old friend. He told me he had been having a drink with one of his work-mates the previous week and he had been talking about the minister in the hospice and how he had 'done the business for ma' faither, last rites an' a' that'. So the word is out! A Church of Scotland minister does a Catholic sacrament for – at best – an agnostic family? No, I don't think so. The truth is that a pastoral need was met in an appropriate way and one family was helped to cope with a death. Was it appropriate? Of course! Would I do it again? Certainly! Was it of God? Absolutely! Was it a sacrament? I have no doubt at all.

DIVERSITY AND INTEGRITY

Is it possible for ministers to respond to the moral and religious diversity of postmodern society in ways which are appropriate and helpful and at the same time maintain their own integrity both as individuals and as ministers? For some ministers there is only one way of maintaining integrity and that is to let people know where they stand and to act accordingly. There are ministers who will not baptize a baby unless the law (of the Church of Scotland) is fulfilled and at least one of the parents either 'joins the church' or attends a class for enquirers. And one can imagine that some Protestant ministers would give a less felicitous response than that in the case study to a request for the last rites. For such ministers integrity involves keeping within the rules and applying them in an even-handed way.

Yet I would argue that there is another way of maintaining personal and professional integrity, and we find an especially good example of this approach in the above story from hospice ministry. First of all Chris, the chaplain, did not discount the request for 'last rites'. He did try (gently) to explain the Roman Catholic context of this rite, but when this made little impact he did not persist. Instead, he offered what was appropriate in his own tradition, namely a reading from the Psalms, the 23rd, and a word of extempore prayer. The fact that what he did was interpreted by the son as 'the last rites' was immaterial. Ministry had been offered and received. In a covering letter which came with the case study the chaplain pointed me to a story in which meeting the needs of the other takes precedence over adherence to the ways of one's own tradition:

The film *The Shoes of the Fisherman* is a portrayal of a Russian dissident priest who ends up becoming Pope. One night he feels out of place in the Vatican. So, in his priest's garb, he takes to the back streets of Rome. He ends up with a doctor friend in the home of a dying man. He moves to the bedside and begins to mouth the words of the Last Rites in Latin. He is hushed by the doctor, who whispers that there are only Jews in the household, not Catholics. Without apology, the priest places his hand over his eyes and begins to chant in Hebrew – a Psalm or a prayer, I do not know which – which he later indicated he had learned in the Russian camps. The family joined in the Hebrew words. The atmosphere is of peace and holiness. And a family were cared for in their needs. Wonderful!

In both case study and film, the object of ministry and its outcome was the bringing of *shalom*. Of such is pastoral integrity amid religious diversity.

THE SCHOOL CHAPLAIN AS COMMUNITY MINISTER

Douglas was minister of an urban priority parish for a number of years. As parish minister he was deeply involved in the local primary school as its chaplain. He describes his ministry in a situation which embraces both the school and a family in his parish.

As the parish minister I am the chaplain to the local non-denominational primary school. The school serves a catchment area which is severely deprived and seen by the church as an Urban Priority Area. Over the course of five years a relationship of trust has been established between me and the headmaster and teachers. I am involved in regular visiting of classes, conducting assemblies, leading the school in church worship at major festivals, and working with classes on topics with religious components. On occasion I have been notified by the school of pastoral need concerning school families.

One such occasion concerned a six-year-old boy named David. Although his behaviour was not causing great concern to the school, he was repeatedly mentioning the absence of his deceased grandfather who had died six months previously. The teacher had made the headmaster aware of this, and both had spoken to David's mother. She was well aware of this 'fixation' and troubled by it. The headmaster mentioned that perhaps the minister would be able to help and the mother willingly agreed that she would like me to call at her home.

After being told of David's situation I arranged to see his mother, Mary, when the boy was at school. I had not visited the home before as the family had no connection with the parish church, though Mary recognized me through my involvement with the school.

Three generations of David's family all shared the one house. David had grown up with the constant background presence of his grandparents along with his mother and father and siblings. His grandmother still lived in the house, and was deeply grieving the loss of her husband. The grandmother was Roman Catholic by background and although she never attended worship the living-room walls were covered in rather garish RC iconography. The funeral was conducted by a non-local RC priest. Mary, however, had an aversion to Roman Catholicism and did not want to have contact with the local RC church.

Mary told me that ever since the funeral David had been constantly referring to his grandfather, and that his behaviour had deteriorated. He would say that he was too sad to go to school, or that his grandfather wasn't there to greet him at the window any more on his return. It had become a real trial to get David to do anything he did not want to do, as according to David this action would run contrary to what his grandfather would have allowed or wanted.

The home behaviour was different from school. Although there he mentioned his grandfather, he was actually compliant with the wishes of his teacher and mixed well with his classmates. In talking with Mary I broached the issue as to whether David was actually using the death of his grandfather as a lever to elicit whatever response he wanted from his family. Mary had thought of this as a possibility but had not had the opportunity to air her opinion. In fact the family as a whole had often referred to the grandfather's continued presence, e.g. 'He is still with us.' They were reluctant to relinquish his being around them.

It was then that Mary talked more about her mother and this widow's inability to let go of her husband. His ashes still remained unburied and were kept in her upstairs room, a fact with which David was well acquainted. Mary was already aware of this prolonged stage of grieving her mother was going through, but again had not had the opportunity to talk to anyone about it. She resolved to face her mother's deep sense of grief and seek ways in which she could help her mother to move onwards. Mary also acknowledged the role the local priest could have in speaking to her mother about her sense of loss and the possible burial of her husband's ashes.

On leaving I gained permission to inform the school of David's home situation. Further, Mary felt better able to cope with David's moods by leading him on in positive ways from his grandfather's absence. She felt more able to come to terms with what was happening around her after talking to someone outwith the family and yet knowledgeable about the school.

In the school, I talked to the teacher and we agreed that it was best that we did not draw attention to David through any specific initiative. To have opened up the subject might have brought the issue back to his mind again, and we felt it best that the 'normal grieving process' be allowed to develop. After the summer holidays it was found that David was perfectly happy at school and that his home life had moved on. Mary was no longer aware of any unduly frequent references from David to his deceased grandfather.

As a chaplain and a parish minister I was aware of the professional boundaries within which I was operating. I was not a child psychologist, and the school certainly did not think that the situation was serious enough to warrant such an input. They saw the minister as a professional who had experience in death, and was therefore qualified to deal with a case which was unusual to them. My chaplaincy allowed me an entry into the family home, while neither provoking nor preventing a change in the relationship the different family generations had to the Roman Catholic Church.

David was helped through the pastoral care of his family and the supportive role of the chaplain and the school staff. Yet at no point was he aware of this background support. The school staff continued to monitor the situation and were willing to consult again and, if need be, more widely in the future should the need arise. Throughout, David was well supported by a loving family and caring school. The chaplain provided the necessary channel with which to bring the care into focus.

SYSTEMS THEORY AND PASTORAL MINISTRY

One way of conceptualizing the work of pastoral care in the midst of complex human situations is in terms of systems theory. The basic presupposition of systems theory is the interconnectedness of people who are not simply isolated individuals but parts of larger networks such as families, schools and communities. One cannot interact with the individual without there being repercussions for the system; neither can one become involved in a system without having some effect upon the individuals who together make up the systems. In his *Generation to Generation: Family Systems in Church and Synagogue* (1985), Ed Friedman has applied systems theory to a study of the interaction between pastors, their families and their congregations. Friedman's thesis is that systems theory offers a far more powerful tool for pastoral ministry than do the theories and techniques of counselling. While a full consideration of systems theory in relation to pastoral care is beyond the scope of this book, three of the key concepts set out by Friedman throw light on the ministry of the school chaplain in relation to David. The first concept is that of the 'identified patient', which suggests that sometimes a person who is diagnosed as being 'sick' or 'disturbed' within a family is really bearing pain for the whole family. (Thus a child who has begun to wet the bed may be bearing the stress of the marital difficulties of the parents, or a woman's drink problem may reflect deeper problems existing within the family.) The second principle is that by working with one person within the system, not necessarily the 'identified patient' and often the person to whom one has easiest access, it is possible to alter what is taking place within the system. The third key idea enunciated by Friedman is the value of pastors being able to intervene in difficult situations with the capacity to be a 'non-anxious presence'.

> Not only can such capacity enable religious leaders to be more clear-headed about solutions . . . but because of the systemic effect that a leader's functioning always has on an entire organism, a non-anxious presence will modify anxiety throughout the whole congregation. (Friedman 1985, 208)

Whether or not Douglas was consciously applying the principles of systems theory is not known, but the case study illustrates how they work out in practice. First, it is easy to see young David as being put in the role of identified patient in the family set-up. While he himself was obviously grieving for his grandfather (who had always been part of his daily life), the whole household was grieving, perhaps not pathologically but certainly acutely – and it cannot have helped a sensitive wee boy to know that his grandfather's ashes were in a box upstairs. Second, Douglas worked with the one person in the family set-up who was accessible to him, namely David's mother. Through this intervention various difficult issues were addressed, such as her mother's inability to 'let go' and the relationship of the family to the RC Church, and Friedman would argue that the improvement in David's behaviour without any direct involvement with the boy can be traced to the minister's conversation with his mother. Finally, what comes through the minister's written account is something of his own non-anxious presence in the situation, of his own comfort in addressing the issues of death and mourning and the relationship between the family and the local Catholic church. Of such is the stuff of parish ministry.

SUPPORTING THE PSYCHIATRIC PATIENT

Elspeth is a parish minister who recently moved to a new charge. She describes her support for a member of her former congregation who has been receiving intensive counselling.

> I think the Church has an important role, not in doing the counselling but in supporting someone who is being counselled. Morag was sexually abused when she was young. I guessed this from a couple of phrases she mentioned to me while she was depressed. I did not tell her or her husband what I thought, but with the help of her doctor got her involved in counselling at the local psychiatric hospital. In the years since then she has been moved on to other counsellors and is now, finally, talking about what happened to her and how she subsequently restructured her life to cope with it. The role I have played is in knowing her parents, who are both now dead (I conducted their funerals), and in supporting her husband. This support has taken many forms. Morag talks to me sometimes in frustration

when the counselling does not seem to be going anywhere. Her husband has talked to me because he often feels excluded both by her and by the counsellors. I remember, for example, when she first told me about one of her symptoms and how her husband knew nothing about this. Together we decided to tell him. I knew that he would respond caringly because I have known them both for such a long time, and was able to give her the reassurance that she needed to tell him. She finds in worship words that help her... I am not always sure what they are. She is a very gentle person who is almost too restrained. When the counsellors have tried to help her express her anger in a safe environment she has come to me and asked how it is possible for Christians to be angry. We have explored together some of the Psalms. Morag maintains that the very beginning of this process was triggered by a sermon in which I said we have to be the same inside as outside. This has been a recurrent theme. She wants to unite her two selves. There is, as she sees it, someone bad inside whom she needs to keep under control. That person she acknowledges may ultimately be her friend and give her back her life but she is very scared of letting it emerge. She is quite dependent upon me, and I know that, but she is intelligent enough to see that dependence for what it is and we are both clear that one day it will come to an end. Meanwhile she still feels she needs to come and listen to me preach (in my new congregation). I am not sure if this has to do with the dependence or because preaching touches the issues that are important to her, such as forgiveness and healing and anger and loss.

ISOLATION AND INTERDISCIPLINARITY

One of the recent classics of pastoral care is *Pastoral Care in the Modern Hospital* (1971) by the Dutch pastoral theologian Heije Faber, a book best remembered for the analogy which he draws between a minister in a hospital and a clown in a circus. Faber identifies three tensions experienced by both minister and clown:

> First the tension between being a member of a team and being in isolation; secondly the tension between appearing to be and feeling like an amateur in the midst of experts; finally the

tension between the need for study and training on the one hand and the necessity to be creative on the other. (Faber 1971, 90)

All three of these tensions are important in pastoral care generally as well as in the hospital, but it is the first which is our present concern. Pastoral ministry can be a lonely business. Despite the theory and theology which locates ministry *within* the community of faith, the reality is that as often as not pastoral care is exercised *on behalf* of that community.

Andrew Irvine has undertaken extensive research into isolation within the parish ministry of the Church of Scotland and some of his findings are summarized in his book *Between Two Worlds: Understanding and Managing Clergy Stress* (1997). He identifies various types of isolation, such as: *geographical isolation*, finding some differences between geographically isolated clergy in the islands and those of the mainland parishes; *professional isolation*, due to the fact that 82 per cent of ministers of the Kirk exercise a solo ministry, although he did recognize some movement to multi-staff ministries; *interdisciplinary isolation*, with a sense of isolation from other professionals in the community who were often caring for the same people; *intraprofessional isolation*, with little support from fellow ministers; *social isolation*, with few friendships outwith the professional context: and *spiritual isolation*, identified as a lack of someone to 'care for the carers'. It has to be recognized that most denominations are aware of these problems and are taking steps to put in place structures to provide better support for ministers (or at least those ministers who are minded to use them).

Our case studies shed an interesting light on two of these dimensions of isolation in particular, namely the intradisciplinary and the interdisciplinary. There was, for Elspeth, a degree of anxiety that Morag was coming some distance from her old parish to her new one to hear her preach, reflecting a concern about crossing parish boundaries and that her action might not be fully approved by colleagues. It is sad that, whatever the reality, these should be the perceptions of colleagues in ministry, though often there is a degree of justification for holding these views. Ministers can be very jealous of their own patch.

From intradisciplinary isolation we turn to what might be regarded as the reverse side of that coin, namely interdisciplinary co-operation. How do our case studies measure up? It is not without interest that interdisciplinary co-operation is integral to the cases presented by the school, hospice and hospital chaplains. These, in fact, tell a different story from that of the professional and personal isolation portrayed in Faber's clown. The chaplains appear to be accepted by their institutional colleagues, whether nurses or teachers, their distinctive role within the team recognized. I think it is arguable that chaplaincy work has changed out of all recognition since Faber was writing thirty years ago. Chaplaincy has changed because it had to. As institutions have made demands for higher skills and greater professionalism from all disciplines, only those in sector ministry who could win professional respect could survive. In the field of hospital chaplaincy (which I know best) appointing bodies would not appoint chaplains whom they did not consider to have the potential for interdisciplinary working. Further, in-service training programmes and the creation of a culture of supervision has led to a general all-round increase in standards in chaplaincy.

Elspeth's support of Morag who was having intensive counselling to help her come to terms with earlier sexual abuse raises for parish (and other) clergy vital issues with respect to interdisciplinary co-operation. From Elspeth's own account it was she who guessed that Morag had unresolved issues in relation to abuse and who in co-operation with her doctor got her into counselling; it is to Elspeth that Morag and her husband keep turning between counselling sessions; and Morag keeps coming back to hear Elspeth preach. The specific details of this story can be related to more general issues with regard to co-operation between ministers and carers in other disciplines.

First, it is often ministers who become aware that there is a problem. This does not mean that ministers are capable of making a diagnosis. They are not. But then neither are nurses or social workers. A definitive diagnosis of a problem should be left to those who have the competence to make it, namely doctors – and even then they sometimes disagree among themselves! Nevertheless, ministers and nurses and social workers, with their own training and experience, will not often be surprised when doctors confirm their 'diagnostic hunches'. What ministers should not do, either openly with the 'client' or even covertly within themselves, is to 'label' someone with a diagnosis, accurate or not. Elspeth picked up a sense of dis-ease linked to sexual abuse. Sensitive ministers may also be among the first to become aware of grief which seems to be going on too long, or of heavy drinking which is beginning to disrupt family life.

Second, it is often an important role for the ministers to refer people for skilled help which they recognize to be beyond their own competence. Having identified the fact that 'there is a problem', the minister may now have a crucial triple role: first, to help the person in trouble to 'own' the problem; second, to create an awareness that help is available; and, third, to invoke within the imagination of the other the thought that he or she can use that help, that life can be better. Referral is a pastoral art. Ministers need to become aware of the limits of their own competence, neither trying to provide help beyond its boundaries, nor referring to a secular therapist when what is required is the support of a minister.

Third, in general, ministers must learn to support without interfering. The accepted wisdom is that, having made a referral or when a member of the congregation is in therapy, the minister should not meddle. There is normally good reason for this. When it is the relationship between therapist and client which is the crucial context for exploring the hurts of the past it is not helpful if the intensity of the therapeutic relationship is diluted by the issues being explored in another arena. Yet sometimes this may be a counsel of perfection or even therapeutically counterproductive. The relationship between minister and client is ongoing. It existed before therapy began and will continue after therapy concludes. In any case, whatever pastoral support means, it cannot be totally vacuous. This does not mean that ministers can provide support without being aware of the dangers of interfering with the therapeutic process. Ideally, minister and counsellor should, with the consent of the client, be aware of what each is doing. Elspeth's pastoral ministry with Morag is a case in point. As a member of her congregation, Morag keeps coming back to her expressing her frustration that the counselling does not seem to be going anywhere. Elspeth has to walk on a tightrope here. On the one hand she has to hear Morag out; on the other hand she must also encourage Morag to take her frustrations about counselling back into the relationship with her counsellor, for only there will progress be made. In this particular case there is one area where Elspeth has a distinctive role as a minister, and hopefully this is a role which Morag takes on in consultation with the counsellor. The issue is Morag's understandable anger. Counsellors had tried to provide a safe environment in which this anger could be expressed, but to no avail. The problem appears to be a religious one. Nice Christian people should not get angry. Elspeth sensitively helps Morag to explore those parts of the Bible, especially the book of Psalms, where the expression of anger is seen as acceptable and normal. Perhaps the problem of the expression of anger has to be laid to rest in the setting which also is the cradle of the problem!

Fourth, ministers must bear in mind the multiplicity of their roles. Elspeth is not only pastor (in the narrow sense of the word), she is also preacher, and Morag keeps coming back to hear her preach, even coming from a distance to her new parish. Elspeth wonders whether there is a dependency problem developing. Perhaps there is, perhaps not. At least both are aware of the possibility and know that one day their pastoral relationship will end. Maybe it is just worth noting that pastoral relationships do not always end neatly with the end of a ministry and that occasionally, and where practical, common sense needs to transcend rigid intradisciplinary boundaries in the interest of good endings. At any rate, Elspeth's preaching has been a significant part of Morag's therapeutic/spiritual journey. The homiletic point about the need 'to be the same inside and outside' triggered something for Morag and set a personal agenda for her, namely to 'unite her two selves'. Perhaps Morag is aware that in Elspeth's preaching there are resources to help her do just that. Since Elspeth is now in a new church it is unlikely that she is even unconsciously writing sermons directed towards meeting Morag's needs. But if the recurrent themes of her preaching are 'forgiveness and healing and anger and loss', then it is not surprising that Morag keeps on coming back in the anticipation that she will find a 'word' for her. We should not underestimate the therapeutic potential of pastoral preaching.

Finally, ministers should be sensitive to the needs of the relatives of someone in therapy. Elspeth is sensitive to the needs of Morag's husband, who has been finding it hard to cope with a wife in therapy. It is not uncommon for counselling to destabilize an otherwise good marriage. In the early stages the therapy may lead clients to regress, taking them into material or aspects of themselves which they cannot share with their spouses. Later in therapy, when progress is being made, the clients may begin to grow, discovering potential within themselves which makes them into different people from those they were before therapy began – or those they were when they were married. Since women are more likely to enter counselling than men, coping with a 'growing' spouse is mainly a man's problem! The pastoral care of the counsellee's spouse has its own challenges, providing support in the midst of a changing relationship and enabling the spouse to 'hang in there' even when not fully understanding the changes which are taking place. It is obvious that Elspeth also had a good relationship with Morag's husband and was doing her bit to prevent him from feeling excluded. Perhaps, at the end of the day, this was not her least important contribution to Morag's therapy.

THE CONTEXT OF CARE

The particularity of these stories demonstrates that there can never be a practice of pastoral care which is de-contextualized or disembodied. The broad context of pastoral care is the real world in all its fragility, the world of family life with its tendency to fragmentation, of work with its threat of redundancy, of media bombardment with its multiplicity of global images. To what extent do the cases described reflect the characteristics of postmodern society as previously described? Perhaps the very fact that I make use of case studies is in itself a reflection of a contemporary understanding that we learn as much from reflection upon particular stories/cases as from stating an argument in abstract terms. Stephen Toulmin (1990) has stressed the importance of communication which emphasized the 'oral, the particular, the local and the timely'. While a written case study certainly does not constitute a form of oral communication, the narrative form itself has a hint of orality about it. We can 'hear' a story being told. Case studies emphasize the particular, the local and the timely.

There is some evidence that new communication technologies themselves are having some impact upon the context in which pastoral ministry is exercised. Elizabeth Henderson (1997) has studied the influence of the portrayal of death in soap opera upon mourning in her own Scottish parish. She has found an increasing tendency for local practices to emulate what happens in the soaps. For example, a friend of someone who had died was pressurized into delivering a eulogy at the funeral (following what had happened in a recent episode of a TV serial). This friend had never spoken in public before and the outcome was disastrous.

A manifestation of the postmodern context of pastoral care is the selection of cases themselves. Of the five cases in this chapter, only Elspeth's supportive ministry to the young woman who was receiving counselling for abuse was firmly located within the context of the local congregation. While four of the five ministers in these cases are parochial clergy (and the other has substantial parish experience), two of them chose to send me an account of a pastoral situation which took place outside the local congregation. While it is possible that this was a conscious, or even unconscious, choice to protect the anonymity of church members, the material itself points to the fact that much pastoral work is carried out at the interface between church and community and among people who would not normally attend worship on a Sunday morning. The stories confirm the postmodern thesis that while traditional modes of religious expression may be on the wane, religious belief, spirituality, the search for meaning (call it what you will) is alive and well. What people respond to is not any authority possessed by clergy by virtue of their office or ordination, but the quality of the pastoral relationship offered, the inner integrity of the pastor.

These different accounts of ministry enable us to identify certain themes which are integral to contemporary pastoral practice. Within the words which have been written down by the ministers there is plenty to engage our interest. Yet it is also arguable that all of these stories 'say more than they say', that there lie within these narratives unspoken assumptions about ministry of a theological nature which are worthy of further exploration.

Within each of the five cases, whether implicit or explicit, there are themes of a theological nature. In a previous chapter I identified certain themes which I maintain are integral to a theology of pastoral care. What one cannot do is to make a straightforward correlation between a theological theme and a given case. Life is not that simple, for the different theological themes are all interrelated and more than one theme surfaces in most of the cases.

INCARNATION AND *AGAPE*

Theologically, proactive pastoral ministry is rooted in *agape*. If the incarnation is an embodiment of divine *agape* accommodating itself to our human condition and meeting us where we are, then likewise proactive pastoral ministry accommodates itself to the human situation of the person to whom pastoral ministry is being offered. In pastoral relationships there is normally a degree of mutuality. Nevertheless, the proactive pastoral carer should recognize that the very fact of making an approach to another person creates, at least initially, a certain imbalance in the relationship. Those who doubt this should reflect upon their own reaction to doorstep evangelists and telephone callers who try to sell them double-glazing. Proactive pastoral ministry must be gentle, not in the interests of the 'hard sell' but out of respect, genuine *agape*, for the other.

In our case studies, the themes of initiative and availability are both explicit and implicit. Anne had been called in to conduct a baptism but everything that followed from that was a result of making herself available to the family as one crisis followed another. Availability is something far deeper than mere physical presence. It is more an attitude to people, a willingness to hear them out, to respond to them out of an awareness of *agape*. It is possible to visit people and not to be 'available' to them because of one's own concerns or personal agenda. This minister was available in every sense of the word – as a minister. It is important to notice, however, that she did not make herself available in her former role as a lawyer.

The theme of initiative and availability is even more explicit in the case of the involvement of Douglas, the school chaplain, in the case of young David. Because he had made himself available to his parish, and in particular to the primary school within his parish, he had built up a network of relationships in which he was trusted – by the headmaster and teachers and by the parents of the children, even by those who were not members of his congregation. It was this trust which led the headmaster to ask for his help, and one can argue that it was the position he had earned for himself in the community which gave him an entrée to David's home. He was known in the parish because of what he had become in the school, and because of this David's mother felt able to trust him. The importance of this should not be underestimated. In the context of a local community, people do not normally ask for 'a minister' (unless any minister will do to bury the dead); in the context of a hospital, patients do not normally ask to see 'a chaplain' (except for a Catholic who may wish to receive some sacramental ministry). When ministers and chaplains are invited into situations, they are normally invited by name because they are known as individuals. The way they have dealt with other situations and what is known of their probable attitude to people and situations is a determining factor in receiving referrals. This is why in a busy hospital, where the potential workload will always far exceed the time available, chaplains are liable to find themselves being used more and more by fewer and fewer wards. Nothing succeeds like success – and absence makes the chaplain totally forgettable.

The story of Chris, the hospice chaplain, also illustrates the themes of initiative and availability. He was called in during the night because he had previously taken the initiative to meet the family of the dying man, probably while visiting in the wards during the day. It is probable too that the night sister had confidence – because she knew him and his way of making himself available to people – that this chaplain, a Presbyterian minister, would not be put out by a request for a Catholic sacrament from a family with no known church connection. This case points to another dimension of pastoral integrity, namely the ability to work ecumenically without losing one's own sense of confessional identity. It is now virtually impossible to exercise a pastoral ministry within narrow denominational boundaries and this is especially true in a hospital or hospice context. The reality of ministry is encounter with people whom one may never have met before, people who bring to that encounter their own belief and unbelief, their factual ignorance and misunderstanding of what they think you believe. 'Setting the record straight' is not appropriate. Yet there is perhaps another kind of integrity, manifested in this story, in discerning the deeper needs being expressed, and responding as appropriately as possible out of an availability rooted in a common humanity. The hospice chaplain is sensitive to the way in which people in a time of crisis find some meaning in symbols and rites even when they appear to have rejected that very institution within which the meaning of these symbols and rites can be best understood. It was certainly rather bizarre for an anti-Catholic agnostic to ask for the last rites for his dying father – and to ask for a Catholic rite from a Presbyterian minister, to boot! Yet at a deeper level something profoundly important was surely going on. The dying man's son wanted to do his best for his father. Nothing more could be done for him in this world, so perhaps something could be done to ease his passing into the next. Was this mere superstition? Or was it a deeper kind of truth of which we only become aware at a time of crisis? When I became a hospital chaplain, an experienced chaplain told me that I would meet no atheists in my new job. He was right, or nearly so. On the boundary between life and death, new realities are perceived, and these realities are sometimes better expressed in symbols and rites rather than words. The hospice chaplain was sensitive to this dimension of human experience and responded in what he believed to be an appropriate, and what later turned out to be a helpful, manner. The fact that the ward sister felt able to call in Barry (also late at night) testifies to an availability which is more than a chaplain's phone number on the duty-room notice board. Elspeth, too, had made herself available to people and this was the basis of her supportive ministry to Morag, who was receiving psychiatric counselling because of sexual abuse. Morag (and her husband) knew she could call on Elspeth at any time and if she were free, Elspeth would respond.

ON BEING AVAILABLE WITHOUT NEEDING TO BE

The near total availability which some ministers offer does raise an important question which needs to be addressed. How do ministers set boundaries to their own commitment, not least because of the need to look after themselves and prevent utter exhaustion? Perhaps there is a need to learn how 'to care and not to care'. In each of the above cases, we see an incarnational ministry taking initiative rooted in *agape*. All of the ministers make themselves available in their own way. Whether visiting in the parish because there has been a bereavement in the family, or called into the hospital or hospice as chaplain, or in the context of an on-going relationship as school chaplain or parish minister, we see a consistent pattern of non-intrusive availability, of the ability to be with someone in need without the need to take over the life of the other. In this we see a reflection of a more profound grace which is available to us but which leaves us with freedom to respond and either accept or refuse what is made available. In none of the cases (as far as we can see) do the ministers depend upon the response in order to confirm their own identity. In *Pastoral Counselling – The Basics*, James Dittes of Yale Divinity School, setting out the core of a lifetime of teaching, reflects upon a pastoral relationship with Alice, a female parishioner:

> As a pastoral counsellor, your principal offering to Alice is a radically focussed and attentive *witness* to her life, made possible by the total renunciation of your role as a 'player' in her life. As pastoral counsellor, you are willing to lose yourself in the sense of being willing to disregard what any of the events

or remarks mean to *you* in order to give your total attention to what they mean to *her* . . . This can't be unlike the experience of grace that derives from an awareness of a God who is willing to sacrifice self-interest for an unrelenting benign self-regard. (Dittes 1999, 11)

Running through the cases there is a persistent attempt to accommodate the pastoral response to the needs of the other, whether through finding the right words or through a holy reticence in the face of suffering. With or without words, grace is communicated, not primarily through words, and certainly not through words alone, but through the quality of the relationship which is offered. In this sense the pastoral relationship is itself parabolic, pointing gracefully beyond itself to the available God.

SUFFERING, DEATH, RESURRECTION AND HOPE

A further feature of the above cases also points, I believe, to the nature of ministry in contemporary society. It was only after I had selected these five case studies and begun to work with them that I realized that in each of them, either centrally or peripherally, there was a death. This was not intentional on my part, for each was chosen for its richness of themes relevant to pastoral care. On reviewing the other cases which I had on file, I discovered that in more than half of them, ministry at a time of bereavement was involved to a greater or lesser extent. One could speculate endlessly about the significance of this. I know some ministers who would claim that in many weeks much of their ministry revolves around taking funerals, and for the majority of them this means pre- and post-funeral visits as well as the service itself. Perhaps it is in ministry to the bereaved that society perceives a clearly defined role for the clergy. And perhaps it is within the context of these societal expectations that the pastoral gifts of ministers find their fullest expression.

Within our cases, we are made aware of the reality of suffering, whether of bereavement or possible infertility or a depressive illness. In the stories told, the themes of crucifixion, resurrection and hope are inextricably entwined. There is no attempt to minimize the pain of those involved. No panaceas are offered. In all of the cases, the pastors stay with the pain. Perhaps they are able to do so because they have all experienced their own Good Fridays and their own Easter Days. We do not know, for it would be quite inappropriate for them to respond to the crucifixion of the other out of their own experience of resurrection. Yet it may well be that it is that very experience which enables them to stay with the pain of the other, to know that there is hope, another way of looking at an awful situation – not now but perhaps later – even when it cannot be changed. As Andrew Lester pointed out (1995, 59), it may be the reality of encountering at a deep level someone who has experienced hope and who embodies hope which itself communicates a hope beyond the reality of present suffering.

What theologically does the pastoral carer bring into such situations? It is arguable that what underpins an ability to minister in situations of human tragedy is a theology of pastoral care which takes seriously the themes of crucifixion, suffering and resurrection. Not that these words can be trotted out as trite platitudes in pastoral conversation at a time of acute suffering. Yet a theology of the atonement which puts an emphasis on the God who is with us and the God who is for us on the cross can at least sustain the pastor in the belief that, even in the most tragic of situations, God is present and there is hope. What is certainly true is that if for the minister there is no vision beyond the limits of a stoic forbearance, then that is what will be communicated, subtly and non-verbally, to those among whom she seeks to minister. It is equally true that if ministry is rooted in the conviction that in the Christian story there is the possibility of new beginnings, then that too will communicate itself in the pastoral conversation.

ROLE AND IDENTITY

In the course of a week ministers will be observed in a number of different roles – leader of worship and preacher, committee chairman and committee member, pastor and community leader, to name only some of the public roles. Concurrently in their private lives, ministers are also spouses, parents, children and friends. This is a reality which distinguishes ministry from counselling. While counsellors may have a number of public roles and share with ministers all the private roles, in counselling there is seldom little contact between counsellor and client apart from their professional relationship, and attempts are usually made to minimize such extraneous contact. In ministry, on the other hand, the multiplicity of public roles is a fact of life, and sometimes even the private roles of ministry are the subject of congregational curiosity. Our case studies amply illustrate the number of different roles assumed in ministry.

At the same time, however, as ministers are required to assume a multiplicity of roles, attention is also being focused upon factors which seem to lead to a loss of ministerial identity. Andrew Irvine in *Between Two Worlds* lists some of these factors. For Irvine, the problem of leading the Church in a post-Christian era is complex. First there are the issues raised by the new information technology:

> In this rapidly changing society the church often continues in practices of yesteryear. Like a horse and buggy on the information highway it relies on yesterday's technology to interface with today's world. The generation of today are faced with a church which communicates its story through written text, lecture-like sermons and a message often totally devoid of relevant visual form. (Irvine 1997, 53)

Second, issues of identity can be related to loss of authority. There are few professions which have escaped this, even medicine. But while doctors are seen to be necessary for survival, 'the church and its leaders have ceased to be viewed by society as speaking with authority to or for the majority' (55). Third, we live in a time of churchless faith. As we saw in our analysis of postmodern society, issues of faith and meaning and value are alive and well – and often outside the Church. In a situation where the Church's contribution to this debate is regarded as minimal if not irrelevant, ministers may seem marginalized with a consequent loss of identity. Fourth, Irvine speaks of a faithless Church and points to a tension which exists within many denominations. On the one hand, there is a move away from theological dogmatism towards social activism, with individuals being encouraged to make their own faith journeys untrammelled by creeds and confessions. On the other hand, there are many people within society searching for certainty, and it is not purely coincidental that the churches which are growing are those which offer this kind of message. Amid such theological polarization ministers need a strong sense of personal identity to survive, let alone function competently. Fifth, there is the issue of relativism, of maintaining a distinctively Christian witness in an increasingly pluralistic society.

> Along with the inclusive and relative world view has come the concept of political correctness. That is to say there is the need to act, speak, organize and model the claims of inclusiveness and relativism. Asserting truth claims can elicit charges for the minister of being politically incorrect . . . The clergy live in the tension between being ministers of the Christian Gospel and living in a politically correct world. (Irvine 1997, 60)

Finally, ministers in their search for relevance, while remaining as ministers of congregations, may invest time and energy in organizations outside the Church, e.g. counselling organizations or political parties. While these activities may be worthwhile in themselves, it may be in these activities that ministers receive most satisfaction and affirmation and consequent sense of identity rather than in their parishes.

Granted that, in our case studies, the ministers were playing a number of roles, what light do these cases throw upon the issue of pastoral identity? On reviewing the case studies, I was struck by the fact that in virtually all of them the ministers were working comfortably in at least two roles. Most commonly there was a pastoral role and a liturgical role, sometimes a private role and a public role. For Anne, her ministry was expressed both in her home visits and in her conduct of the baptismal and funeral services. For Douglas, it was his public role as school chaplain which allowed him to exercise a private pastoral role with the mother of the grieving six-year-old. Chris, the hospice chaplain, moved easily from pastoral conversation into a mutually acceptable version of the 'last rites'. In the case of Elspeth, supporting a member of her congregation who was having counselling, both the home visits and her preaching were important ingredients in pastoral care. And we can guess that the request to Barry that he conduct the funeral of the stillborn baby had everything to do with his visit to the grieving parents.

Perhaps the truth is that in none of these situations were the ministers 'role-playing'. The success of their ministry lay in the fact that each of them was the same person in each situation. Pastoral identity (and pastoral integrity) consists in not playing roles but in being oneself, in being genuine or 'congruent' (to use the Rogerian term). Ministers face a crisis of identity precisely when they begin to play roles, or (in Jungian terms) to adopt a 'persona', to put on a mask. There are some ministers who are comfortable in one-to-one relationships but find difficult the 'public performance' of a sermon or funeral service. Perhaps they share the doubts and uncertainties of those who sit before them in the pews and can offer no easy comfort. Sometimes their integrity leads them from ministry into other ways of helping people. Other ministers have a 'gospel to proclaim' but do not find it easy to get into deep personal relationships. They function by adopting the 'persona' of the pastor and are seldom helpful. It is arguable that there can be no effective pastoral ministry, no pastoral care of integrity, unless ministers have to some degree integrated their private and their public selves, unless they are the same person in their pastoral care as they are in the pulpit. In Chapter Four we noted Brueggemann's assertion that the 'truth' of the biblical narrative was central for pastoral care. We read also of his belief that it is the telling of the Christian story *and* the celebration of the liturgy which provides the material to fund the imagination and enable pastoral care to be transformative of human life. In all of our cases we see, either explicit or implicit, a unity of word and being shaped by the Christian story. We see care expressed with consistency in both the private pastoral relationship and the public act of worship.

CHURCH, MINISTRY AND PLURALISM

Throughout these case studies there is an implicit theology of the Church and an understanding of the permeable nature of the boundary between Church and world. In Anne's case, ministry was with people who lived in the parish. She went initially in response to a request for baptism and found herself in a situation of ever-increasing complexity. The criterion for ministry was not membership but need. In the cases of Chris (the hospice chaplain) and Douglas (the school chaplain), we see Presbyterian ministers offering a pastoral relationship to Roman Catholics, again on the basis of need. And again boundaries are managed with grace. Throughout the case studies we see a very broad understanding of the nature of the Church, help being offered in ways which affirm the integrity of the other's faith community. In the case of Elspeth supporting Morag, who was having psychotherapy, we see a minister affirming the integrity of the secular therapeutic process, not in competition with it but confident of her own role. The ability to work across boundaries, whether confessional or professional, should not be considered evidence of a lack of sense of identity, or of thinking that such boundaries do not matter. Rather, there is implicit here a theology of the Church which is defined by its centre and not by its boundary. In each of the above accounts of ministry, it is arguable that each ministry can work on the boundary because their own identity has at its centre a theology funded by the Christian narrative. It is this which gives both personal and professional identity to those involved in the kind of ministry which can offer pastoral care amid the diversity and pluralism which constitute postmodern society.

We must take seriously Andrew Irvine's perceptive analysis of the loss of identity among the clergy. Yet there may be more to be said. The Church must certainly improve its modes of communication in an age dominated by information technology. It is also true, however, that in a 'high tech' society there remains a place for the intimate pastoral relationship, especially in a time of personal crisis. Granted that the authority of the ministry is now questioned as never before, we must also recognize that while there is certainly a loss of authority which can be ascribed to role, there is another kind of authority based upon the person of the minister which can be used creatively and pastorally. The fact of 'churchless faith' means that a great deal of ministry will be exercised beyond the bounds of normal congregational life, but this is no new experience in situations where the locus of ministry has traditionally been the parish or community rather than simply the local congregation. The ambiguities of faith and doubt, the polarities of dogmatism and indifference, experienced both within and outside the Church, call for ministers who have come to some sense of their own identity. This is not an identity based upon absolute certainty but an identity which is comfortable with ambivalence, with knowing and not knowing. It is an identity in which identifying questions may be more important than providing answers. It calls for an understanding of pastoral ministry which has its own identity and integrity in a postmodern world.

In this chapter, five ministers have described and reflected upon examples of their own pastoral practice. I have attempted some further reflection upon the cases. I have also suggested that pastoral care in a postmodern world requires that ministers must be reflective practitioners. In the next (final) chapter I shall explore further the concept of reflective practice and its relevance for pastoral ministry in postmodern times.

CHAPTER EIGHT

Pastoral Care as Reflective Practice

At the beginning of the book I stated my intention to 'reaffirm the contribution of the Church's traditional ministries of pastoral care to the healing and health of individuals and communities'. By 'traditional ministries' I mean those ordained to the ministry of Word and sacrament, whether full-time or part-time, paid or non-stipendiary. This has been at the core of my own 35-year-long journey in ministry as a practitioner and teacher of pastoral care. I recognize how my perspective is shaped – maybe even distorted – by that experience. This perspective has also dictated the selection of case material set out in the previous chapters, all of it from ordained ministers, Presbyterian and Episcopalian, both full-time and part-time. My experience, and that of the ministers upon whose work I have drawn, is part of the reality of the Church as it is now and is in the process of becoming. The pastoral role of the ordained ministry has its own integrity. Yet it is an integrity which only exists in the context of a wider integrity, namely that of the ministry of the whole Church. In Chapter One I also spoke of the renewed emphasis upon the ministry of the whole people of God. This has been brought into even sharper focus in the current emphasis upon Collaborative Ministry, one of the key concepts in the recent Report on the Theology and Practice of Ordination (Church of Scotland 2000).

THE CONTEXT OF ORDAINED MINISTRY

The Committee which produced this report was set up partly as an attempt by a reconstituted Board of Ministry to clarify what it was about and partly in response to the decline in the number of people offering for the ordained ministry. It was realized that there was no point in mounting a recruitment campaign until there was some clarity and agreement about the kind of ministry for which they were being recruited. Widespread consultation took place within the Church, with other churches and with many outside the Church who still value its contribution to the common life of the nation.

First, theological principles are set out congruent with both the Reformed tradition and current ecumenical thinking. The primary ministry is the ministry of Jesus Christ in the world; the mission and ministry of the Church is to participate in that ministry of Jesus Christ in the world. Within this context of the ministry of the whole people of God and the bestowal of different gifts for that ministry, there are some who are called to exercise a distinctive ministry of Word and sacrament. One purpose of this particular calling is to keep open the possibility of Church reform and renewal in our time.

> God has gifted the ordained ministry of the Gospel to his Church to represent Christ in the faithful proclaiming of the Word and the right administration of the Sacraments and so ensure the possibility of such reform and renewal. As the Church wrestles with questions of structural reform and spiritual renewal today it needs a ministry whose calling is to keep before it the Gospel of Jesus Christ in all its fullness. (Church of Scotland 2000, 17/10)

Second, the report seeks to describe the kind of society within which ministry and mission must take place. The words used are not much different from any description of postmodern society. Contemporary Scotland (like the rest of the United Kingdom) is in a process of rapid change, becoming increasingly secular, pluralist and mobile. The Church must not respond by falling into the 'nostalgia trap', looking backwards to a romantic past and forwards to a bleak future. Neither is there a single solution, a magic wand which can be waved, to solve all the problems which face the Church. The Church must respond creatively and with understanding rather than reacting defensively to a changing society.

The Committee which produced this report was convened by William Storrar, Professor of Christian Ethics and Practical Theology in the University of Edinburgh. We see the kind of understanding called for in his contribution to a collection of essays marking the publication of new liturgies by the Church of Scotland and the Presbyterian Church in the United States. Storrar's essay is an analysis of the social context of the worship of the Church of Scotland.

> In the now notorious pick and mix culture of personal believing without corporate belonging, and in a post-mass production economy, the Church of Scotland is still struggling on as a characteristically modern institution, with its central bureaucracy, heavy investment in buildings and low investment in the education and training of its members and dependence on a full-time ministry...
>
> Contrary to the many theories of secularisation which suggest that the advent of modernity inevitably undermines the Church and erodes Christian faith, I believe that the Church of Scotland made a brilliant accommodation with the modern world. For the best of missiological reasons it married modernity...
>
> In so many ways the Church of Scotland enjoyed a long and happy marriage with modernity. It is precisely the relatively sudden collapse of the modern world which has left it grief-stricken in the widowhood of postmodernity...As a grief reaction to what was a sudden and unexpected cultural and social change, the Church of Scotland is currently caught in the unhealthy reaction of denial, depression and repressed anger, rather than the healthier process of what Arbuckle calls grieving for change, finding a new life and purpose after the loss. (Storrar 1999, 78)

One task, therefore, of the ordained minister is to help the Church grieve for a past which has gone and move on to a different kind of life in the future. Pushing the metaphor a little further, it must be recognized that caring for the bereaved has its own impact upon the carers.

> Ministers will have to be people who can cope creatively with the impact of a changing Scotland on their own lives and ministry. In such a society ministers are clearly subject to change, uncertainty and stress. (Church of Scotland 2000, 17/13)

Yet those who care for the bereaved know also that grief does not

have to go on for ever, indeed that grief without end is pathological, and that for most people there is life beyond sadness,
almost certainly a different life but one with its own satisfactions
and challenges.

A PROFILE OF ORDAINED MINISTRY

It is the above context, the care of people and communities in
transition, which shapes the pastoral task and the selection and
preparation of those called to it. The report does not seek to be
prescriptive on this matter but sets out a profile of the gifts
necessary for ordained ministry. Those called and ordained
must possess maturity of faith, sound judgement, healthy self-
awareness and sensitivity towards the needs of others. Their
manner of life must be a manifest demonstration of the
Christian gospel; they must exhibit personal integrity in all
aspects of life; their lives must be marked by the fruits of the
Spirit and lived in communion with God. Who would dare read
this list and offer him or herself as a candidate for ministry?
Which one of us now in ordained ministry comes anywhere near
living up to this high vision? There is, however, an element of
healthy realism as well.

> Ministers of the Gospel share a common humanity with their
> neighbours and a common discipleship with their fellow
> Christians. They are not superior human beings or special
> Christians, but frail and fallible people always dependent on
> the renewing grace of God. And yet, in those called to this
> particular ministry, the Church should discern a mature and
> growing integration of person and practice, being and func-
> tion, as two related aspects of the one life lived in Christ's
> grace and service. (Church of Scotland 2000, 17/18)

'A mature and growing integration of person and practice, being
and function . . .' Here we are at the heart of pastoral integrity. If
such integrity cannot be imparted by education and training,
perhaps it can be recognized and nurtured. It is about self-awareness, being in touch with both strength and weakness, with both
ability and vulnerability; it is about knowing a little but not
knowing (or even having to know) everything; it is about taking
risks when to do nothing is to take a risk as well; it is about
making a decision not because it is absolutely right but because

you think it is the best one in the circumstances – and then living with the consequences even when it turns out to be wrong. All this is about doing ministry in a particular way. It is about the process of becoming and continuing to be 'reflective practitioners'. It is arguable that these two words, 'reflective practitioners', are the end-point of the Church of Scotland report as well as the goal of ministerial formation. The words were not invented by the authors of the report. They have a significant, if short, history within a wider sphere of professional education. I now wish to use them as an integrating concept in seeking to pull together the various arguments which I have made so far. There is, however, an important prior question. What is the relationship between the pastoral task of the ordained ministry and the ministry of the whole people of God?

COLLABORATIVE MINISTRY AS THE CONTEXT OF REFLECTIVE PRACTICE

While the phrase 'collaborative ministry' may be newly minted, the idea is not. Theologically its roots are in New Testament thinking about the ministry of the whole people of God. It means to work together. In terms of contemporary ministry, the term 'collaborative ministry' brings together a constellation of other terms which describe the organization of ministry today. There are certain things which the term does not mean. It does not mean lay people helping 'ministers' to do their jobs. Nor does it mean the abolition of the difference in function between ordained and lay. Whatever else the 'priesthood of all believers' means it does not mean that every Christian becomes a priest in his or her own right. In the New Testament, priesthood is primarily corporate, shared. Positively it is possible to say the following about collaborative ministry:

- Collaborative ministry begins from a fundamental desire to work together because we are all called by the Lord to be a company of disciples, not isolated individuals.
- Collaborative ministry is committed to mission. It is not simply concerned with the internal life of the Church. Rather, it shows the world the possibility of transformation, of community, of unity within diversity.
- Collaborative ministry does not happen just because people

work together or co-operate in some way. It is a gradual and mutual evolution of new patterns.

- Collaborative ministry is built upon good personal relations highlighting the importance of emotional maturity.
- Having the courage to face and work through conflict, negotiating until a compromise is found, and seeking help to resolve it, are not weaknesses, but signs of maturity and commitment.

Collaborative ministry is not a single thing. It takes different forms in different places – team ministries within a given congregation, involving people with different ministries, ordained and/or lay; group ministries involving a number of congregations, sometimes ecumenical or interdenominational; institutional ministries in which the chaplain either functions as a member of an interdisciplinary team or does not function at all. The days of the one-(wo)man-band are over. This kind of ministry demands new skills of the ordained minister, both to participate in and to provide leadership for new patterns of working together – and perhaps a different kind of spirituality as well.

What, then, of the model of pastoral ministry which is central to this book? It could be argued that most of the cases have an individualistic flavour to them and that they are somewhat anachronistic in the context of the kind of collaborative ministry to which I have alluded. My basic response is that collaborative ministry does not render redundant the intense kind of pastoral care which belongs properly within the one-to-one relationship. In fact, many of the cases described have been brought forward by ministers working in team ministries. I also know that ministers of Word and sacrament find themselves routinely in pastoral situations of great intensity. This happens not only because they are normally full-time and therefore find themselves in pastoral situations more frequently than lay pastors. The pastoral office itself provides a context in which many people turn for help. Yet at the heart of the pastoral office there can be an essential loneliness which is not fully assuaged even when the minister is part of a collaborative ministry. The loneliness of bereavement or loss or anxiety or distress on the part of the cared for can be equalled by the loneliness or the inadequacy or vulnerability of the carer. Whatever developments take place in new patterns of ministry, there will remain demanding pastoral tasks to be undertaken, tasks which themselves will need to be reflected upon for the sake of future ministry.

There is therefore at the heart of ordained ministry a tension. On the one hand, the ministry of the ordained is contextualized, theologically and practically, within the life and ministry of the whole people of God; on the other hand, pastorally and practically, ordained ministers find themselves at the sharp end of situations in which women and men are experiencing great distress and to which they are required to respond by virtue of their pastoral office and according to their abilities. Afterwards, ministers can reflect upon such events in one of two ways. They either learn from their experience or they do not. Yet 'learning from experience' is easier said than done. Speaking at the General Assembly of the Church of Scotland some years ago, Dr Ed White, then associated with the Alban Institute in Washington, said, 'Some ministers have 40 years of experience, others have one year's experience 40 times over.' In order to learn from experience one must become a reflective practitioner.

THE REFLECTIVE PRACTITIONER

The concept of 'reflective practice' was conceived and developed by Donald Schoen, Professor of Urban Studies and Education at Massachusetts Institute of Technology. In two books (1983, 1987) he uses the concept to explore both how theory relates to professional practice and the nature of professional practice itself. His thesis is that there is a fundamental fallacy at the heart of much professional education, a fallacy which concerns the theory–practice relationship. He argues against the assumption of 'technical rationality' which assumes that there is a standard body of knowledge which can be learned in professional schools and then applied to a range of issues 'out there' in the work situation (a position against which I have already argued as we explored the story of the inarticulate ordinand in Chapter Two). Schoen's seminal insights have found resonance among a range of professional disciplines. They have been drawn upon by Jackson Carroll as a basis for reflecting upon the practice of ministry. Carroll takes as his starting point the inadequacy of professional education for ministry, with its assumption that the academic learning in seminary is sufficient in itself to produce competent, functioning ministers. What is learned in seminary may be valuable, perhaps even essential, but it is not enough.

Carroll argues for a re-thinking of the professional model of ministry based upon four assumptions. First, the Church is a community which provides, through its gathered life, a context in which people find meaning, belonging and empowerment; second, the ministry of the Church is the task of the whole people of God; third, sharing the ministry does not imply a sameness of function for all Christians; fourth, the primary ministries of lay persons are not in the gathered life of the Church but in its scattered life (Carroll 1986, 15).

Carroll, therefore, affirms the distinctive role of the ordained minister in the life of the Church, but it is different from the traditional one. He finds his new model in the concept of reflective practice as set out by Schoen:

Schoen's discussion of this alternative understanding of professional practice is derived from observation and analysis of the ways that competent practitioners from several different professions confront difficult situations of practice, situations for which there are no ready made answers or standard repertoire of techniques that can be applied in a relatively unreflective manner. From his observation and analysis, he found a somewhat similar pattern or method of professional practice across the professions when practitioners confronted complex, unusual situations. The pattern which he calls 'reflective conversation with the situation' includes the following elements which are brought variously into play by reflective professionals

- Skills in analysing a situation one is confronting in an effort to frame the problem and understand what the issues are.
- Values or 'appreciative systems' which also aid in framing the problem and evaluating and reflecting on the situation as one proceeds.
- Overarching theories which supply language and themes for making sense of phenomena in the situation.
- An understanding of the professional's own role in the situation, both its limits and its opportunities.
- The ability to learn from what Schoen calls 'talkback' from the situation one acts in, learning from the situation and adjusting one's practice in the light of this 'talkback'.
- Willingness to treat one's clients – or in the clergy's case, one's parishioners – as 'reflective practitioners' as well, with knowledge, insights and abilities which contribute to the solution of the problem in hand. (Carroll 1986, 23)

PASTORAL CARE AS REFLECTIVE PRACTICE

In the preceding chapters I have included about 15 examples of contemporary pastoral care sent to me by ten different ministers. Let us now revisit them to see how far they are the work of reflective practitioners. I shall attempt to do so in terms of the six bullet points listed above, but first I must make two cautionary points. First, we should not expect every case to be illustrative of every one of the points. Life – and ministry – is not that neat. Indeed, the attempt to fit all the cases into one interpretive mould is precisely what one cannot do. Schoen's concept of the reflective practitioner must not become the new 'grand narrative' of pastoral theology! Second, when they were invited to send me case material, my colleagues in ministry were not asked to impose any interpretation upon it, let alone one derived from current thinking about reflective practice. In fact some case material was submitted which included personal reflection of considerable depth and upon this I have drawn. I have also in this book included material of different kinds in my own reflection upon the cases submitted. This means that in the paragraphs which follow I will be working with two levels of analysis, the first-hand reflection of those directly involved in the cases and my own more distant and second-hand reflection upon both the cases and the more immediate reflection of my colleagues.

Let us then see to what extent the cases described are congruent with Schoen's elements of reflective practice.

SKILLS IN ANALYSING A SITUATION

Since those who submitted case material were not asked for their own analysis we can only accept as a bonus that which was provided. Three ministers in particular are quite explicit in their attempt to frame the problem and understand what the issues are. We find this capacity first of all in Ruth, as she seeks to conceptualize what has really been happening to Jim, the young man subjected to homosexual rape (p. 46). She understood and 'held' his deep-seated anger against his parents alongside the positive knowledge she had of his family; she drew upon her own family history to help her understand what was going on without disclosing that in a way which would not have been helpful; she was sensitive to 'the visible moment of disclosure' when Jim's outlook began to change. Significantly (using Schoen's exact word) she states 'a new frame for both our lives was opened up . . .'

Barry's account of his late-night visit as hospital chaplain to the parents of a stillborn baby (p. 136) is almost a running commentary of his analysis of the situation. He demonstrates his understanding of the actions of the sister, the distress, ambivalences and differing emotional reactions of the grieving parents and his sensitivity to the fact that one grandfather was a minister.

Elspeth, too, as she describes her role in support of Morag who was in psychotherapy (p. 147) is very perceptive in her framing of the relevant issues. She suspects there may be a background of abuse and picks up hints of depression. She realizes the limits of her own competence and guides Morag into counselling without giving the appearance of abandoning her. She is aware of the problem of dependency, and that awareness helps her cope with it. There is an understanding of Morag's anger which leads on to an appropriate use of the Psalms. It is worth noting that 'Elspeth' is also the minister who took the funeral of the young woman who had been brutally murdered by her former husband (p. 85). In this story we find the same kind of attempt to reflect upon what was going on, particularly regarding the request for a church funeral.

We find this capacity for analysis also in the three stories provided by Frank as he seeks to reflect upon his ministry in the context of the postmodern city. He understands Paula's need for a 'semi-detached' association with the congregation; he is aware of 'ministry on the hoof'; he does not attempt to convert Colin from Buddhism to Christianity but is aware of the complexity of the ways in which people believe; at the same time he ministers out of a conviction about the truth of the gospel, a Story which has shaped his story but which he does not need to impose upon others; he understands the social pressures which have brought Derek and Gillian, 'homeless, jobless and penniless', to his door.

I believe that we could consider all of the cases described in the previous chapters and find in them some attempt, either explicit or implicit, at framing the problem (which may of course be a result of being asked to write about them!). One further point is worth noting. In no case is there any dogmatism in the analysis. Elspeth does not hesitate to express her uncertainty. She is not sure what Morag finds helpful in worship, nor whether her former parishioner's continuing visits to her new parish are related to dependency issues. She never was completely sure why the parents of the murdered woman wanted a service in the church. Likewise, Barry 'sought not to provide answers but to encourage Brian and Kathleen to explore the depth of their questions'. Yet neither Elspeth nor Barry allow ministry to be inhibited by uncertainty. They have enough understanding on which to take action but that action is always liable to be modified by new insights. In the same way Frank, in his ministry to the homeless couple, is aware of the risk he is taking. 'It means taking the risk of being let down rather than taking the risk of becoming cynical' but 'it is my risk'. Such is the nature of reflective practice.

VALUES OR 'APPRECIATIVE' SYSTEMS

For Schoen, this means that reflective practitioners cannot function without a system of values. For us this means a theology of pastoral care. Schoen maintains that reflective practice cannot take place other than within a set of values, an understanding of what it means to be a professional who is a human being in relationship with other human beings. It is of the very nature of pastoral care that it is rooted in a value system, indeed a theology which the pastor believes provides a basic framework for ministry. In our exploration of models of ministry (premodern, modern and postmodern) we have already explored the rich diversity of ways in which a theology of pastoral care may be expressed. Yet within that diversity there is fundamental agreement about issues which constitute that theology, issues such as the nature of God and the nature of the Church and its ministry.

Implicit within all 15 case studies there is a belief in a God who is gracious and in ministry as a reflection, however imperfect, of that grace. Pastoral initiative is rooted in the divine initiative, and the former like the latter is non-intrusive, leaving space for people to respond as they will. We see the divine grace manifested in the healing words to the lady elder whose unmarried daughter had become pregnant; we see the divine availability made manifest in the chaplains who went to their hospital or hospice when they were needed; we see that grace – and a deep understanding of the nature of the Church and its sacraments – expressed in the ministry of the hospice chaplain who ministered so freely across denominational boundaries.

In previous chapters I have tried to expound in some detail the implications for pastoral care of the story of Jesus Christ, believing that the events in that story shed further light on the nature of ministry. Each of these events have their own importance but it is an importance derived from faith in a gracious God. It is an understanding of the cross and resurrection of Jesus the Son as integral to the grace and love of God the Father which makes it possible to minister with hope in situations of devastating loss. It is a belief in the Spirit of God who goes before us which enables us to take risks and proceed with courage into those situations where we 'partly know and partly do not know'. Values and beliefs are foundational for the reflective practice of pastoral care.

OVERARCHING THEORIES

Schoen argues that reflective practice requires overarching theories which supply language and themes for making sense of phenomena in a situation. Our case studies do not provide explicit evidence of this, which is not surprising since it was not asked for. It is, however, implicit in some of the cases. This is particularly so in relation to understanding the nature of loss and the need for ritual to help people come to terms with their loss. Elspeth's funeral service in the church for the sake of the parents of the woman who had been murdered, Anne's two services, a baptism and a funeral, in the complex family situation she described, Barry's ministry to the parents of the dead baby, Chris's ministry of 'last rites' to the lapsed Catholics, all point to this grasp of the nature of grief and the importance of ritual. This is the kind of grasp which for many professionals has become second nature, intuitive and part of their being, rather than a theoretical concept mechanically applied.

In Chapter Seven I introduced some theoretical material as a way of possibly deepening our understanding of the inner dynamics of some of the situations described. In considering the ministry of Douglas, the school chaplain, with young David whose grandfather had died, I suggested that a grasp of family systems theory could help us to understand the importance of his interaction with Mary, the boy's mother. While David was the 'identified patient' it was Mary who was pastorally accessible and through whom he could minister to the whole family, including David. I also introduced Andrew Irvine's research on 'isolation in the parish ministry' as a way of shedding light on ministers in their relationships, with both colleagues and themselves. The value of such theoretical perspectives is not that they provide a blueprint for describing how things ought to be. Rather, they provide a conceptual framework for understanding things as they are. Where the theory does not match reality, the theory will be modified or deepened. Such is the use which the reflective practitioner will make of 'overarching theories'. They must not be elevated to the status of 'grand narratives'.

AN UNDERSTANDING OF THE PROFESSIONAL ROLE

Schoen highlights the need for the reflective practitioner to be aware of his or her own role in the situation, of both limits and opportunities. Pastors run the risk of neglecting both limits and opportunities. At one extreme there are ministers who can be somewhat messianic and attempt to work in situations clearly beyond their knowledge and skill (I say this notwithstanding my previous statement that sometimes risk-taking is a necessary part of ministry). At the other extreme there are ministers so unsure of their role that they function with a timidity which fails to grasp opportunities. Again the ministry of Douglas, the school chaplain, provides a good illustration. He comments that 'as a chaplain and a parish minister I was aware of the professional boundaries within which I was operating. I was not a child psychologist, and the school did not think that the situation was serious enough to warrant such input. They saw the minister as a professional who had experience in death and was therefore qualified to deal with a case which was unusual to them.' Elspeth, too, in her support of the woman having psychotherapy, demonstrated a real awareness of both limits and opportunities. She was aware of the difference in professional role between her and the psychiatrist. On the one hand she was careful not to muddy the relationship between the woman and her therapist; on the other hand she was aware that there was a distinctive contribution she could make in helping Morag to reconcile her anger with her Christian faith. Further, Elspeth was aware of her distinctive role in supporting Morag's husband. Such constant awareness of limitations and possibilities is part of what it means to be a reflective practitioner.

LISTENING TO 'TALKBACK'

Schoen points to the need to learn from the situation as one acts in it, adjusting one's practice in the light of this 'talkback'. For an example of this we turn to the story of the Anglican deacon who was hesitant about whether or not to bless the dying woman

(p. 57). Here we see a woman deacon learning from the situation, realizing how absurd her scruples must seem in the eyes of God. Perhaps, too, the words 'You can't win them all', coming from the minister who prayed for life when the patient wanted death (p. 54) is the kind of 'talkback' which can come when one does all the right things for the right reasons – and is misunderstood. In such situations one must still listen to the 'talkback' but not necessarily change one's practice.

TREATING OTHERS AS REFLECTIVE PRACTITIONERS

Schoen identifies the need to treat others as reflective practitioners who have knowledge, skills and abilities which contribute to the solution of the problem at hand. It is arguable that the primary task of supervision is to help trainees become reflective practitioners. So, to return to the case of the inarticulate ordinand with which I introduced Chapter Two, the task of supervision was not to supply him with the words which he did not have, nor was it to tell him what he ought to have done. Rather (to recapitulate the previous five points) it was to help him first, to analyse the situation and understand the reason for his inability to find words; second, to help him to affirm the value of the Christian story as he had discovered it in his life and in his studies (though not to 'apply' it in a simplistic way); third, to help him find some deeper understanding of what sickness and hospitalization might mean to people; fourth, to help him begin to articulate his own understanding of the role of a minister with both its limits and its opportunities; and fifth, to reduce his anxiety and sense of failure to the extent that the particular situation could 'talkback' to him, enabling him to grow in ministry. While this particular story relates to a minister in training, the ability to engage in what Schoen calls 'reflective conversation with the situation' is a requirement of on-going ministry.

REFLECTIVE PRACTICE AND LIFE-LONG LEARNING

We have already explored two of the main concepts set out in the Board of Ministry report of 2000. These are 'a collaborative approach to ministry' and 'a reflective practice of ministry'. A third key concept is also identified, namely 'a commitment to formation in ministry'. This applies not only to the education and training of those destined to become ministers of Word and sacrament; it applies also those called to other commissioned ministries of the Church such as deacons and readers. It must also be the theme which underlies the whole adult education policy of the Church, for all are called to participate in on-going collaborative ministry. And it applies not only to initial formation but also to continuing education, and nowhere more so than in relation to the ordained ministry.

> As those called and ordained to the ministry of Word and Sacrament, ministers of the Gospel in the 21st century must be reflective practitioners, collaborative leaders and formative learners . . . The theology and practice of ordained ministry affirmed here . . . requires a clear capacity and commitment among all ministers of the Gospel to deep reflection, genuine collaboration and continuing formation as persons in Christ and practitioners in ordained ministry. (Church of Scotland 2000, 17/24)

The report is clear on the issue of 'continuing formation'. Life-long learning will more and more become part of the normal experience of ministry, as in other professions. I have sought to demonstrate the attributes of reflective practice by reference to the cases made available to me by colleagues in ministry. Almost without exception these were ministers whom I knew to be involved in some kind of continuing professional education, sometimes at Master's level (and in one case at the level of the professional doctorate). I am not arguing that they became reflective practitioners because of their advanced studies in ministry (though I would like to think these helped). Rather, I am arguing that their reflection upon their current practice of ministry led them to see the need for some kind of structure to help them develop what they were already doing. Continuing education (not necessarily at degree level) will, I believe, play an increasingly vital role in the support and development of the ordained ministry, in increasing the capacity of reflection and in decreasing levels of stress and the sense of isolation.

TOWARDS A REFLECTIVE PASTORAL PRACTICE FOR POSTMODERN TIMES

In Chapter Six I drew upon the work of James Fowler to set out three models of ministry corresponding to the premodern, the modern and the postmodern temper. In order to function as a pastor in postmodern times it is not necessary or even desirable to buy into all the philosophical presuppositions of postmodernity; rather, one must be able to function effectively and with integrity in a postmodern culture. Perhaps it is not stretching the argument too far to say that the minister for postmodern times is essentially a reflective practitioner. I pointed to the need for such a pastor to have a deep understanding of the pressures which impinge upon the lives of people today; Schoen pointed to the need for skills in analysis and for theoretical understanding which would supply a language and themes making more sense of situations. Throughout this book I have sought to affirm the central role of the Christian story as an interpretive framework for pastoral care; Schoen focuses on the need for values or 'appreciative systems' which help to frame problems as well as evaluating and reflecting upon the situation. My primary concern has been a reaffirmation of the role of the ordained minister in pastoral care; Schoen made a plea for an understanding of the professional's role in the situation. My use of case studies has been one method of demonstrating how we can learn by reflecting upon experience, both our own and that of others: Schoen highlights the need to listen to talkback and adjust one's practice in the light of what is heard. In reaffirming the role of the ordained ministry I have done so in the context of an understanding of collaborative ministry, the ministry of the whole people of God; Schoen points to the need to treat clients (and – adds Jackson Carroll, in the case of the clergy – parishioners) as reflective practitioners with knowledge, insights and abilities which contribute to the solution of the problem in hand.

We see, therefore, very clear parallels between the kind of pastoral ministry which is now required and the concept of reflective practice. This leaves one final question to be addressed. In Chapter Two I pointed to the deficiencies of an earlier model of pastoral care which found itself captive to the philosophies and practices of the then current secular psychotherapies. Is there now a danger that, in advocating a reflective practice model for pastoral care, ministry could find itself in a similar captivity to a professional model which might have relevance for other disciplines but which is not appropriate for ministry?

REFLECTIVE PRACTICE AND PASTORAL INTEGRITY

The answer to the question at the end of the last paragraph must be that it could happen but that it need not do so. It is possible for ministers to become so infatuated with a secular model of practice that they neglect their primary commitments and eventually find themselves divorced from them. The process by which this can happen has been well described by the Whiteheads (p. 28f.). Its principal means of prevention must lie in what the Board of Ministry report identifies as 'the integration of person and practice in ordained ministry'.

Such integration of person and practice is, for me, another way of talking about spirituality. I have not said much about spirituality so far, not because I do not think it important but because I believe it to be implicit in my whole argument. It is a curious fact that the twentieth century, the century of science and technology, should see at its end a burgeoning interest in spirituality in many different manifestations. Only time will prove the continuing value of each. Whatever else spirituality means for the ordained minister, it must mean finding some anchorage for his or her own story within the Christian story, a story to which he or she relates on a continuing basis. That relationship will be nurtured by the kind of devotional life which each individual finds fulfilling. It will also find focus in regular worship either as celebrant or participant. Men and women are not simply 'called and ordained': they are 'called and ordained to the ministry of Word and sacrament'. Pastoral care is an activity which has as its larger context the life and worship of the Church where the Word is preached and heard and, in the sacraments, that Word is made visible. This is the spiritual context of reflective practice. In an article on 'calling' in other professions, James Gustafson writes:

> A 'calling' without professionalization is bumbling, ineffective and even dangerous. A profession without a calling, however, has no taps of moral and human rootage to keep motivation alive, to keep human sensitivities and sensibilities alert, and to nourish a proper sense of self-fulfilment. Nor does a profession without a calling easily envision the larger ends and purposes of human good that our individual efforts can serve. (Gustafson 1982, quoted in Carroll 1986, 28)

If this is true of the so-called secular professions, how much more true is it of the profession of ministry? There is only one thing worse than having a conceptual theory for ministry which one must use with caution, and that is having no conceptual framework at all. It is not unknown for the adjectives 'bumbling', 'ineffective' and 'dangerous' to be applied to ministers! However (to misquote Viktor Frankl), while we can have our theories, we must not allow our theories to possess us. In other words, any conceptual theory must be baptized in the service of ministry. It must be our servant, not our master.

In the above quotation, Gustafson is setting out a secular understanding of 'calling'. The calling which sustains ordained ministry is precisely the same calling which sustains the whole people of God in their collaborative ministry in both Church and world. It is the call to discipleship, to learn from the experience of participating in the story of Jesus Christ. It is participation in this story which keeps alive the vision and the motivation for ministry; it is this which helps to maintain sensitivity to human suffering and need; it is this which provides the fulfilment in ministry which comes when it is least expected; it is this which helps us to locate pastoral care within and as part of that larger purpose which is the coming of the kingdom of God.

The integrity of pastoral care is not a concept which can ever be totally made flesh. For the ordained ministry, which is the particular focus of our exploration, the phrase embodies a series of tensions within which pastoral ministry must be exercised. There is the tension between being a member of the body of Christ and being called to a particular ministry within that body; there is the tension between theology and practice, of relating one's deepest convictions to the realities of each situation; there is the tension of knowing something but not knowing enough – and taking decisions on the basis of the former; there is the tension between vision and achievement, of being 'good enough' rather than perfect. True integrity in pastoral care means ministering with courage in the midst of these tensions. Dietrich Bonhoeffer in his *Ethics* points to the difference between the 'ultimate' and the 'penultimate'. To the penultimate belongs all our human activity, our theorizing and our theologizing, our attempts at pastoral ministry and our feeble spirituality, our flashes of insight and our pretentiousness. To the ultimate belongs only the Word of God. When all is said and done, pastoral care finds its true integrity in the realm of the ultimate, in the grace which transcends and encompasses our striving.

Bibliography

Ballard, P. and Pritchard, J. (1996), *Practical Theology in Action*. London, SPCK.

Barth, K. (1963), *Evangelical Theology; An Introduction*. London, Collins Fontana.

Bauman, Z. (1995), *Life in Fragments: Essays in Postmodern Morality*. Oxford, Blackwell.

Bonhoeffer, D. (1955), *Ethics*. London, SCM.

Bonino, J. M. (1997), 'Liberation Theology', in McGrath, A., *Christian Theology: An Introduction*. Oxford, Blackwell.

Bowden, J. (1983), 'Narrative Theology', in *New Dictionary of Christian Theology*. London, SCM.

Bright, J. (1960), *A History of Israel*. London, SCM.

Browning, D. S. (1976), *The Moral Context of Pastoral Care*. Philadelphia, Westminster.

Browning, D. S., ed. (1983), *Practical Theology: The Emerging Field in Theology, Culture and World*. New York, Harper & Row.

Brueggemann, W. (1991), *Interpretation and Obedience: From Faithful Reading to Faithful Living*. Philadelphia, Fortress.

Brueggemann, W. (1993), *The Bible and Postmodern Imagination*. London, SCM.

Buckroyd, J. (1996), Review of *Counselling in the Pastoral and Spiritual Context*, in *Journal of the British Association for Counselling*, Vol. 7, No. 4, p. 332.

Campbell, A. V. (1985), *Paid to Care: The Limits of Professionalism in Pastoral Care*. London, SPCK.

Campbell, A. V. (1986), *Rediscovering Pastoral Care*, 2nd ed. London, Darton, Longman and Todd.

Capps, D. (1984), *Pastoral Care and Hermeneutics*. Philadelphia, Fortress.

Capps, D. (1995), *Agents of Hope*. Minneapolis, Fortress.

Carr, W. (1985), *Brief Encounters: Pastoral Ministry Through the Occasional Offices*, London, SPCK.

Carr, W. (1997), *Handbook of Pastoral Studies*. London, SPCK.

Carroll, J. W. (1986), *Ministry as Reflective Practice: A New Look at the Professional Model*. Washington, Alban Institute.

Carroll, J. W. (1991), *As One With Authority: Reflective Leadership in Ministry*. Louisville, Westminster/John Knox.

Church of Scotland (2000), *Ministers of the Gospel: Report of the Board of Ministry to the General Assembly of the Church of Scotland*. Edinburgh, Church of Scotland.

Clebsch, W. A. and Jaekle, C. R. (1964), *Pastoral Care in Historical Perspective*. New York, Harper Torchbooks.

Couture, P. D. and Hunter, R. J., eds (1995), *Pastoral Care and Social Conflict*. Nashville, Abingdon.

Cox, H. (1965), *The Secular City*. New York, Macmillan.

Cox, J. T. (1964), *Practice and Procedure in the Church of Scotland*. Edinburgh, Blackwood.

Crites, S. (1971), 'The Narrative Quality of Experience', in *Journal of the American Academy of Religion*, pp. 291–311.

de Gruchy, J. W. (1987), *Theology and Ministry in Context and Crisis*. London, Collins.

Dittes, J. E. (1961), 'Psychology and a Ministry of Faith', in *The Ministry and Mental Health*. New York, Association Press.

Dittes, J. E. (1999), *Pastoral Counselling: The Basics*. Louisville, Westminster/John Knox.

Dockery, D. S., ed. (1995), *The Challenge of Postmodernity: An Evangelical Engagement*. Wheaton, Ill., Victor Books.

Dror, G. (1997), 'Riches, Rivalries and Responsibilities in the Pastoral Counselling Setting', in *Papers of the 6th European Conference on Pastoral Care and Counselling*, Ripon.

Erickson, E. (1965), *Childhood and Society*. London, Penguin.

Faber, H. (1971), *Pastoral Care in the Modern Hospital*. London, SCM.

Farley, E. (1983), *Theologia: The Fragmentation and Unity of Theological Education*. Philadelphia, Fortress.

Farley, E. (1990), 'Practical Theology, Protestant', in Hunter, R., ed., *Dictionary of Pastoral Care and Counseling*. Nashville, Abingdon.

Foskett, J. and Lyall, D. (1988), *Helping the Helpers: Supervision and Pastoral Care*. London, SPCK.

Fowler, J. W. (1981), *Stages of Faith: The Psychology of Human Development and the Quest for Meaning*. New York, Harper & Row.

Fowler, J. W. (1987), *Faith Development and Pastoral Care*. Philadelphia, Fortress.

Fowler, J. W. (1995), 'The Emerging New Shape of Practical Theology'. Unpublished paper, International Academy of Practical Theology.

Fowler, J. W. (1996), *Faithful Change: The Personal and Public Challenges of Postmodern Life*. Nashville, Abingdon.

Frankl, V. (1988), *The Will To Meaning*. New York, Meridian.

Freeman, A. (1993), *God In Us: A Case for Christian Humanism*. London, SCM.

Friedman, E. (1985), *Generation to Generation: Family Systems in Church and Synagogue*. London and New York, Guilford.

Freud, S. (1905), *Three Essays on the Theory of Sexuality*. London, Penguin, Freud Library Vol. 15.

Fromm, E. (1950), *Psychoanalysis and Religion*. New Haven, Yale.

Gerkin, C. V. (1984), *The Living Human Document: Re-Visioning Pastoral Counseling in a Hermeneutic Mode*. Nashville, Abingdon.

Gerkin, C. V. (1991), *Prophetic Pastoral Practice*. Nashville, Abingdon.

Gerkin, C. V. (1997), *An Introduction to Pastoral Care*. Nashville, Abingdon.

Goodliff, P. (1998), *Care in a Confused Climate: Pastoral Care and Postmodern Culture*. London, Darton, Longman and Todd.

Graham, E. L. (1993), 'The Sexual Politics of Pastoral Care', in *Life Cycles*. London, SPCK.

Graham, E. L. (1996), *Transforming Practice: Pastoral Theology in an Age of Uncertainty*. London, Mowbray.

Gustafson, J. (1982), 'Professions as Callings', in *The Social Service Review*, Vol. 56, December, p. 514.

Halmos, P. (1965), *The Faith of the Counsellors*. London, Constable.

Hay, D. and Hunt, K. (2000), 'Is Britain's Soul Waking Up?', in *The Tablet*, 24 June, p. 846.

Henderson, E. M. (1997), Unpublished MTh dissertation, Edinburgh University.

Hiltner, S. (1949), *Pastoral Counseling*. Nashville, Abingdon.

Hiltner, S. (1958), *Preface to Pastoral Theology*. Nashville, Abingdon.

Hiltner, S. (1972), *Theological Dynamics*. Nashville, Abingdon.

Holifield, E. B. (1983), *A History of Pastoral Care in America*. Nashville, Abingdon.

Holifield, E. B. (1990), 'Tillich, Paul', in *Dictionary of Pastoral Care and Counseling*. Nashville, Abingdon.

Holloway, R. (1997), *Dancing on the Edge*, London, Fount.

Houlden, J. L. (1983), 'Biblical Theology', in *New Dictionary of Christian Theology*. London, SCM.

Hunsinger, D. van Deusen (1995), *Theology and Pastoral Counseling*. Grand Rapids, Eerdmanns.

Hunter, R. and Janson, M. (1990), 'Cross and Resurrection', in *Dictionary of Pastoral Care and Counseling*. Nashville, Abingdon.

Hurding, R. (1998), *Pathways to Wholeness: Pastoral Care in a Postmodern Age*. London, Hodder and Stoughton.

Irvine, A. R. (1997), *Between Two Worlds: Understanding and Managing Clergy Stress*. London, Mowbray.

James, W. (1900), *The Varieties of Religious Experience*. London, Fontana (1960).

Jones, C. (1996), 'The good, the bad and theology', in *Tomorrow Is Another Country: Education in a Postmodern World*. Church of England Board of Education.

Kendrick, S. (1992), 'On Spiritual Autobiography: An Interview with Frederick Buechner', in *The Christian Century*, 14 October, pp. 900–4.

Klink, T. (1966), 'Supervision', in Fielden, C. R., ed., *Education for Ministry*. Dayton, Ohio, American Association of Theological Schools.

Kohlberg, I. (1976), *Collected Papers on Moral Development*. San Francisco, Harpers.

Lambourne, R. A. (1974), 'Personal Reformation and Political Formation in Pastoral Care', in *Contact: The Interdisciplinary Journal of Pastoral Studies*, Vol. 44.

Lawrence, D. H. (1960), *Lady Chatterley's Lover*. London, Penguin.

Lartey, E. Y. (1996), 'Practical theology as a theological form', in *Contact: The Interdisciplinary Journal of Pastoral Studies*, Vol. 119.

Lartey, E. Y. (1997), *In Living Colour: An Intercultural Approach to Pastoral Care and Counselling*. London, Cassell.

Lester, A. (1995), *Hope in Pastoral Care and Counseling*. Louisville, Westminster/John Knox.

Lindbeck, G. A. (1984), *The Nature of Doctrine: Religion and Theology in a Postliberal Age*. Philadelphia, Westminster.

Lyall, D. (1993), 'Edinburgh 1979 – Thirteen Years On', in Becher, W., *et al.*, eds, *The Risks of Freedom*. Manila, Pastoral Care Foundation.

Lyall, D. (1995), *Counselling in the Pastoral and Spiritual Context*. Buckingham, Open University Press.

Lyall, D. (1999), 'Pastoral Counselling in a Postmodern Context', in *Clinical Counselling in Pastoral Settings*. London, Routledge [1995 Frank Lake Memorial Lecture, Clinical Theology Association, Oxford].

Lyall, D. (2000), 'Pastoral Care as Performance', in *Blackwell Reader in Pastoral and Practical Theology*. Oxford, Blackwell.

Lynch, G. (1997), 'Towards a Narrative Perspective on Pastoral Care and Counselling', in *Clinical Theology Association Newsletter 70*, Oxford.

Lyotard, J.-F. (1984), *The Postmodern Condition*. Manchester, Manchester University Press.

McDonald, J. I. H. (1989), *The Resurrection: Narrative and Belief*. London, SPCK.

McGrath, A. (1994), *Christian Theology: An Introduction*. Oxford, Blackwell.

McLendon, J. (1974), *Biography as Theology*. Nashville, Abingdon.

McNeill, J. T. (1951), *A History of the Cure of Souls*. New York, Harper & Row.

Menninger, K. (1973), *Whatever Became of Sin?* New York, Hawthorn.

Middleton, J. R. and Walsh, B. J. (1995), *Truth Is Stranger Than It Used To Be: Biblical Faith in a Postmodern Age*. London, SPCK.

Moltmann, J. (1974), *The Crucified God*. London, SCM.

Moseley, R. M. (1990), 'Liberation Theology and Pastoral Care', in *Dictionary of Pastoral Care and Counseling*. Nashville, Abingdon.

Muir, E. (1956), 'The Incarnate One', in *One Foot in Eden*. London, Faber & Faber.

Muncie, J. *et al.* (1995), *Understanding the Family*. London, Sage/Open University Press.

Northcott, M. S. (1990), 'The Case Study Method', in *Contact: The Interdisciplinary Journal of Pastoral Studies*, Vol. 103.

Nouwen, H. (1972), *The Wounded Healer; Ministry in Contemporary Society*. New York, Doubleday.

Nouwen, H. (1977), *The Living Reminder*. New York, Seabury Press.

Pattison, E. M. (1972), 'Systems Pastoral Care', in *Journal of Pastoral Care*, Vol. XXVI, No. 1.

Pattison, S. (1988), *A Critique of Pastoral Care*. London, SCM.

Pattison, S. (1997), *Pastoral Care and Liberation Theology*. London, SPCK.

Patton, J. (1983), *Pastoral Counseling: A Ministry of the Church*. Nashville, Abingdon.

Piaget, J. (1950), *The Psychology of Intelligence*. London, Routledge and Kegan Paul.

Rad, G. von (1957), *Old Testament Theology*. London, SCM.

Randall, R. L. (1979), 'What Do You Say After They Say "We're Living Together"?' in *Journal of Pastoral Care*, Vol. XXXIII, 1 March, pp. 51–9.

Ricoeur, P. (1981), *Hermeneutics and the Human Sciences*. Cambridge, Cambridge University Press.

Robinson, J. A. T. (1963), *Honest to God*. London, SCM.

Rogers, C. R. (1951), *Client-Centered Therapy*, Boston, Houghton Mifflin.

Rogers, C. R. (1961), *On Becoming A Person*. Boston, Houghton Mifflin.

Sampson, P., Samuel, V. and Sugden, C., eds (1984) *Faith and Modernity*. Oxford, Regnum Books.

Schleiermacher, F. (1830), *Brief Outline of the Study of Theology*. Richmond, John Knox Press (1966).

Schoen, D. (1983), *The Reflective Practitioner*. New York, Basic Books.

Schoen, D. (1987), *Educating the Reflective Practitioner*. San Francisco, Jossey Bass.

Scott, T. (1977), 'Ministries in the Secular Arena', in *Contact: The Interdisciplinary Journal of Pastoral Studies*, Vol. 56.

Stacey, N. (1971), *Who Cares*. London, Hodder and Stoughton.

Steele, L. (2000), 'An Experiment in Biblical Practical Theology: Reflections on James Fowler's Theory of Faith Development in the Light of Ephesians 4:11-16'. Unpublished paper given at Conference on 'The Use of the Bible in Pastoral Practice', Cardiff, June.

Stokes, A. (1985), *Ministry After Freud*. New York, Pilgrim Press.

Storrar, W. (1999), 'From *Braveheart* to Faint-heart: Worship and Culture in Postmodern Scotland', in Spinks, B. D. and Torrance, I. R., eds, *To Glorify God: Essays on Modern Reformed Liturgy*. Edinburgh, T. & T. Clark.

TeSelle, S. (1975), 'The Experience of Coming to Belief', in *Theology Today*, Vol. XXXII, pp. 159-60.

Thompson, T. (2000), 'Counselling for victims could be more hindrance than help', in *The Scotsman*, 6 January.

Tillich, P. (1951), *Systematic Theology*, Vol. 1. Chicago, University of Chicago Press.

Tillich, P. (1952), *The Courage To Be*. London, Fontana.

Toulmin, S. (1990), *Cosmopolis: The Hidden Agenda of Modernity*. Chicago, University of Chicago Press.

Tracy, D. (1981), *The Analogical Imagination: Christian Theology and the Culture of Pluralism*. New York, Crossroads.

Truax, C. B. H. and Carkuff, R. R. (1967), *Toward Effective Counseling and Psychotherapy*. Chicago, Aldine.

Tucker, G. M. (1990), 'Old Testament and Apocrypha, Traditions and Theology of Care', in *Dictionary of Pastoral Care and Counseling*. Nashville, Abingdon.

Underwood, R. L. (1993), *Pastoral Care and the Means of Grace*. Minneapolis, Fortress.

Whitehead, J. D. and Whitehead, E. E. (1975), 'Educational Models in Field Education', in *Theological Education*, American Association of Theological Schools, Vol. XI, No. 4.

Whyte, J. A. (1973), 'New Directions in Practical Theology', in *Theology*, Vol. 76.

Wilson, M. (1985), 'Personal Care and Political Action', in *Contact: The Interdisciplinary Journal of Pastoral Studies*, Vol. 87.

Wise, C. (1951), *Pastoral Counseling: Its Theory and Practice*, New York, Harper.

Wright, G. E. (1952), *God Who Acts*. London, SCM.

Index